MW00973676

The Five Marks of a
DISCIPLE

The Five Marks of a
DISCIPLE

Be One – Make One

JOEY RODGERS

XULON PRESS

Xulon Press
2301 Lucien Way #415
Maitland, FL 32751
407.339.4217
www.xulonpress.com

© 2021 by Joey Rodgers

All rights reserved solely by the author. The author guarantees all contents are original and do not infringe upon the legal rights of any other person or work. No part of this book may be reproduced in any form without the permission of the author. The views expressed in this book are not necessarily those of the publisher.

Unless otherwise indicated, Scripture quotations taken from the Holy Bible, New International Version (NIV). Copyright © 1973, 1978, 1984, 2011 by Biblica, Inc.™. Used by permission. All rights reserved.

Printed in the United States of America

Paperback ISBN-13: 9781662811814
Ebook ISBN-13: 9781662811821

DEDICATION

To my wife, Meg, for her steadfast
faithfulness to the Lord, to our marriage,
and to our family.

In memory of two of the greatest men
I have ever known: My life mentor, hero,
and Grandpa, Frank Italo Berta, and
my spiritual mentor Carl Dobson.
I am grateful for their investment
of Jesus in them into me.

TABLE OF CONTENTS

PREFACE

If you aim at nothing, you will hit it every time.
Zig Ziglar

I MUST CONFESS, I am not very good at darts, or cornhole, or many leisure activities that require hitting a target or bull's eye. In fact, I find such games rather frustrating, because I think I should be better at them than I am. What is even more frustrating is losing to people at these games when I believe I should win (yes, I am a little competitive). Basketball is not my game either. My now 14-year-old son beats me at H.O.R.S.E. on a regular basis. While he is a basketball player for his school, he is too young to be beating his dad at anything. Right?

In darts, everyone wants to hit the bull's eye. In cornhole, the goal is to get the beanbag through the hole. In basketball, the objective is similar, the target is the basket; and to win you must shoot the ball through the hoop. For me, in darts, I am just happy to hit the target much less the bull's eye. In cornhole, let's just say that if I hit the board, I am happy! And in basketball, can you say "Air ball?" Actually, it is not that bad..., it is more often a "brick." Point being, one's aim is important. This is true in ministry as well. The aim of the Christian life is Jesus; and the Great Commission is the method Jesus invites us to endeavor to make disciples of all nations.

It is to this calling that I have a burning conviction I have to address. I am compelled to speak up and shout it from the mountaintops – even if only ten people listen. For deep within my heart, after 30-plus years in full-time ministry, I can say with great conviction that the results of our ministry efforts, by and large, have not produced the results we have been aiming to achieve. When Jesus called us to *go into the world and make disciples of all nations,* I cannot help but think that He had something else in mind than what we have today. Suffice to say, based on the evidence, we have missed the mark. While most pastors and churches valiantly set out to make disciples of all nations as Jesus commanded, we have wound up, at best, making churchgoers and trying to keep the spiritual masses entertained and satisfied. The question is why?

I fear we have aimed at nothing and hit the bull's eye. I am certain we set out to make disciples without knowing exactly what a disciple is, even though Jesus clearly showed us. Yet based upon the current spiritual condition and climate of our churches and culture, the sad evidence testifies that we have produced something, but it is not a genuine follower of Jesus. Now, this does not mean there has not been a courageous attempt to return the church back to its mission of making disciples of all nations. Thankfully, there is! Nor does it mean that making disciples is not at the forefront of our thinking – it is! Nonetheless, the proof is in the proverbial pudding. We have churches filled with good people, enjoying good programs and preaching, but whose lives are more apt to live for the American dream than for the Kingdom of God. We have far too many people professing faith in Christ whose lifestyles and tendencies testify to the contrary.

To be fair, we have gotten here because we continue to perpetuate what we have learned from those who have gone before us whether or not it was accomplishing the mission. It reminds me of the story of the husband sitting at the kitchen table while his wife prepared a ham for dinner. As the story goes, after the husband watched his wife cut off about one inch from either end of the ham, he asked why she cut the end off. She replied, "It is because that's the way my mom prepared a ham." The husband then asked, "Why did your mom cut the ends off?" The wife confessed that she did not know. Of course, later, the wife called her mom to find out why she cut the ends of the ham off, and her mom's response was, "Because that was the way my mom prepared ham." A few weeks later at a family event, the wife asked her grandmother why she cut the ends off of the ham?" Smiling, she said, "So that the ham could fit in the baking pan."

Do we really know why we are doing ministry and church the way that we are doing it today? More importantly, do we know why? As I ask these questions, please understand that I am neither throwing stones nor casting blame, but I am just calling it like I see it. By all appearances, one of the biggest reasons we are not making disciples is because we apparently do not have a clear picture of a biblical disciple. Churches and church leaders appear confused on the topic. As I have learned, if you get a hundred Christians and church leaders in a room and ask them to define disciple, at minimum, you will hear at least one more answer than people present.

With this in mind, while this writing might be categorized within the genre of discipleship, it is more about what is a disciple than how to make a disciple. We have to know what we are aiming at if we are actually going to hit it. With this in mind, we must be warned that unless we biblically define what a disciple is, we might just be pouring new wine into an old wineskin. Lest we forget, a Jesus-follower is defined by Scripture, not by church culture or the latest denominational trend. Therefore, we must identify and qualify exactly what a disciple is through Scripture before we set off on the journey to make one. Furthermore, until we identify and define a disciple, we cannot fully determine the best pathways to making what Jesus called us to make — a fully developing follower of Himself.

As I have wrestled with this idea, I have come to the conclusion that we need to look at this through a different lens. If I were charged with taking a group of people on a trip, it would be extremely helpful if I first knew the destination. Not only would it help to determine the route, it would also assist in determining the means. For example, if we are headed to Seattle from Atlanta, not only are there a variety of routes to consider, but we would have multiple options regarding the mode of travel. Are we going to travel by plane, train, or automobile? If I am traveling from

Atlanta to Chattanooga, it would be silly to go by plane. Suffice to say, knowing the destination makes all the difference.

The same is true in making a disciple. If we do not know the destination of what a disciple is, then no matter which route we take, we will never know if we have ever arrived. I fear too many ministers and ministries have spent years wandering in the wilderness of ministry, massaging our programs and curriculum, only to wind up catering to churchgoers, and not actually seeing lives transformed into Great Commission followship of Jesus. So, to make us feel good about ourselves, we have been forced to alter the scorecard in exchange for something less than God's expectation. In fact, by all indications, it appears we have learned the art of making church attenders, but not so much making disciples. We have performed ministry on the basis of our common sense instead of upon His calling and mandate. As a result, we all know of churches, pastors, and churchgoers whose spiritual lives are frustrated and broken down on the side of the road to becoming a disciple.

Consider what Oswald Chambers penned so many years ago on March 4, in *My Utmost for His Highest*, "It is easier to serve God without a vision, easier to work for God without a call, because then you are not bothered by what God requires; common sense is your guide, veneered over with Christian sentiment. But if once you truly hear the full commission of Jesus Christ, the awareness of what God wants will be your goal from that point on, and you will no longer be able to work for Him on the basis of common sense."[1] Oh how we so desperately need a fresh wind to blow out the dust within to return us to a ministry based on calling instead of common sense.

This brings me to the genesis of this book. It all began over forty years ago when a layman named, Carl Dobson, took me under his wing and invested the Jesus in him into me to encourage me to maturity in the faith. Simply put, Carl discipled me. He taught me how to know and walk in an abiding relationship under

---

[1]   Oswald Chambers, *My Utmost for His Highest*, (Grand Rapids: Discovery House, 1963), March 4.

the influence of the Holy Spirit. He taught me how to study and apply the Scriptures to my life, how to pray, how to share my faith, and how to be a faithful steward of God's blessings in my life. While I am indebted to other men like Gary Hollingsworth, Glenn Dyer, Steve Wilson, John Rushing, and a host of incredibly patient friends in ministry who have helped to shape my spiritual and ministry life, without a doubt, no one person's life has had a more prolific impact upon my life than Carl's.

Another contributing factor occurred a few years ago when I was asked to host a pastor's roundtable at the North America Mission Board. Joined by twenty-seven other pastors, we took an afternoon to discuss the topic of making disciples. In the course of our conversation, that centered more on making converts and churchgoers than true disciples, I was compelled to ask a simple question. How many of you (pastors called to equip the saints and to lead their church in making disciples) have had a person take you under their wing and pour the Jesus in them into you? How many of you have been discipled? The answer shocked me. Out of twenty-eight pastors present, including me, only three had ever been discipled. THREE! And one of them was a friend who also had been discipled by Carl.

Do you see the problem? How is the Church to accomplish the mission of making disciples of all nations when those who have been called to lead this missional movement have never been discipled themselves? Can you say, "Houston... we have a problem!" In fact, since that day, as I have continued to engage with other pastors, I continue to find that the vast majority of pastors and church leaders have never been discipled. NEVER! Maybe this is why our churches and ministries are struggling in the mission; could it be that we actually do not know what a disciple is and have defaulted to making converts and churchgoers? We have been aiming at nothing and hitting it!

With this in mind, my hope in this writing is to have us all step back, take a deep breath, and identify what a disciple is, so that maybe, we can begin charting a new course that actually accomplishes our Lord's mission of making disciples of all nations. One thing is certain, if we continue on the same course we have been on, we are only going to perpetuate the definition of *insanity*. Hopefully, this book can be a catalyst for breaking the cycle and bringing encouragement to us all.

FORWARD

Foreword by Dr. Rob Peters

THERE ARE TWO words in the Christian vocabulary every believer must attempt to define. The way we ascribe meaning to these two words will determine the substance and shape of our Christian experience. Because most Christians have never stopped to define these two words and develop these two concepts, they remain in the dark about the essential desires God has for this world. The two words that demand being defined are church and disciple. Let me attempt to start the conversation by providing definitions.

A church is a baptized body of believers gathering to worship God, study the Bible, share the gospel, receive the ordinances, and encouraging believers to become disciples of Jesus Christ while living together on mission for Him.

A disciple is a person who spiritually lives life daily in ways compatible with the life and teachings of Jesus Christ. This requires knowledge and understanding of biblical teachings, but ultimately, being a disciple involves the lifestyle and habits that flow out of a daily relationship with Jesus Christ.

At the heart of these definitions are the final and comprehensive mandate Jesus gave to His church – to make disciples. All four gospels conclude with Jesus' clearly expressed mandate to make disciples; however, the entire content of each gospel is an expression of what it looks like to make disciples as Jesus discipled His own disciples. If this has been Jesus' final mandate and Great Commission, why has it not been the absolute focus of the local church?

I have stood in room after room with senior pastors for the past five years, and I have consistently asked one question as a part of our church revitalization ministry, "How many of you have been discipled by someone who intentionally developed you into a follower of Jesus?" In many rooms no hands are raised. In every room no more than twenty-five percent of hands are raised. In most rooms, ten percent of hands are raised. Why is it that Jesus' explicit command and clear example have been betrayed? How can the church recover its disciple-making focus?

In his book, The Five Marks of a Disciple, Dr. Joey Rodgers has unpacked clearly and biblically a framework for a true disciple. Dr. Rodgers has added to the corpus of works, a definitive book on disciple-making that has been shaped in the crucible of local church life and ministry. This book is not detached from the local church, nor does it have as its goal the development of an idealized philosophy. This book is intensely practical and can help every un-discipled pastor and church leader to discover what it means to be a disciple, as well as help every over-programed church rediscover what a discipleship culture must entail.

I can say without question that Dr. Rodgers is one of those rare breeds who was discipled and who was taught that disciple-making lies at the heart of the Christian mission. He understands that the Christian life is not developed by a program or curriculum, but through life-to-life interaction where believers truly engage one another at the point of need. As such, his church is defined by the five marks he writes about, and the members of his church reflect the image of Jesus and the life He lives through them. Likewise, Dr. Rodgers has designed the church he leads around the five marks of discipleship, and the culture is a noticeable contrast to the consumer, corporate, and club models he writes about in chapter four.

Make no mistake, there is an allure to an authentic, joyful, hopeful, loving disciple of Jesus Christ. You will discover the appeal of the life of a disciple as found in these five marks. I invite you into an old type of discipleship book that many new types of churches must rediscover.

Dr. Rob Peters
Peachtree City, GA

CHAPTER 1

ONE MISSION

Only a disciple can make a disciple.
A.W. Tozer

ONE OF MY most embarrassing moments occurred on the football field when I was in ninth grade in a game against our arch-rivals. Tasked with the responsibility of catching and returning punts, I assumed my position on the field in the waning moments of the game with my team winning by six points. As the ball was launched into the air, and with my eyes fixed on the ball in flight, I recall taking a couple of steps back to position myself for the catch. Then, as any good returner would do, I took my eyes off the ball momentarily to survey the field and the on-coming defenders to determine if I needed to call for a fair-catch or if I could return the kick – and then it happened! When I returned my eyes to find the ball, it was nowhere to be found. Instead of seeing pigskin, all I could see was the sun – that is, until the ball landed right on top of my helmet. Yes, the ball hit me square on the top of my helmet, bouncing ten feet back up into the air, landing inside our ten-yard line to be recovered by the opposing team. Then, to make matters worse, two plays later, our rivals ran the ball in for a touchdown costing my team the game. Needless to say, this was not my finest moment.

In that moment I had but one job... CATCH THE BALL! I did not have to run with it or pass it off to another teammate; all I had to do was catch it. Instead, I momentarily took my eyes off my mission and lost the ball in the sun, costing my team the game – all because I lost sight of my objective and did not keep the main thing the main thing.

In Matthew 28:19-20, we discover the final recorded teaching of Christ, better known as the Great Commission. In this passage, Jesus commands His followers to *go into the world and make disciples of all nations.* And now, for some 2000-plus years, God's church has been trying to live out this commission of winning people to faith in Christ, growing them to maturity in the faith, so they can be sent out into the world to make more disciples. Sounds simple, right? Yet often, by all appearances, one has to wonder how we are doing at the task. Is it possible we have misinterpreted the mandate and have lost the forest for the trees? Is it possible that we have taken our eyes off the mission just long enough to survey the landscape of life, only to lose our commission in the name of doing church? Is it possible we unintentionally have inverted Jesus' model for making disciples in our desire to make converts?

SOME PERSPECTIVE

I was born into a semi-religious, morally average family. My parents were loving, hardworking, and present, yet not overly spiritually minded. As a result, the few religious experiences I encountered were inconsistent and motivated more out of expectation or tradition than an intimate pursuit of Christ. In fact, while I am certain the name of Jesus was expressed in my household, the single memory I have of church was a Sunday school teacher declaring to my class, "You are what you eat!" And another child exclaiming, "Oh God..., I'm a chicken leg!" Thus, the day David Whiting sat beside me at my brother's baseball game in Dresden Park to speak with me about God's love for me still resonates as the first time I can recall really hearing the name of Jesus. David was a junior in high school and a committed Jesus follower. I remember how he asked a few penetrating questions to attain a sense of my spiritual condition before explaining the amazing work of Christ on the cross to pay for my sins. I also still remember the conviction I experienced when he asked if I wanted to pray

2

to invite Jesus into my life to be my Savior and Lord. While I did not accept Christ's invitation that day, it planted the seed and launched me on a journey that would ultimately lead to my acceptance of Christ as my Savior.

Shortly after meeting David, he invited me to participate in a number of outings with other middle and high school age students. It was through events like ice skating, roller skating, and go-carting that I was introduced to Carl. Carl was quite the character. With his half-tucked shirt, unkempt hair, and *Western Sizzlin'* diet, Carl was a modern-day cross between John the Baptist and the apostle Paul. He was also the catalyst for what might have been the largest, multi-site student ministry anywhere in the country outside of the church. Weekly, Carl was teaching three Bible studies with eighty-five plus students in three locations and individually discipling twenty to thirty people. His spiritual influence easily exceeded twenty schools in the metro Atlanta area. Here is what you need to know about Carl – he was bold and convinced in his faith. Carl was constantly asking spiritually loaded questions and engaging in evangelistic dialogue with anyone he could gain an audience. Truly, there is no telling how many students and adults he influenced to Christ and personally discipled in the faith. All I know is – I am one of them.

After several months of attending social events and Bible studies where I was hearing the gospel taught and explained through Carl and his band of spiritual misfits, I was invited to go to camp at Florida Bible College in Hollywood, Florida. During the week, as I focused more on girls than Jesus, I continued hearing about God's love and grace which eventually led to a crescendo of conviction to receive Christ as my Savior – and still, I resisted. Thankfully, Carl and his gang were patient. One of the things I appreciated most about Carl was he never forced the issue of faith. He explained the truth, laid out God's plan, and left the results to the Holy Spirit. As a result, a couple of weeks after camp, I awoke one morning with an insurmountable sense of conviction that I needed to give my life to Christ. Because Carl had so thoroughly explained the plan of salvation and the conviction of the Holy Spirit, I knew in that moment God was speaking to me. So, at the age of 12, I slid out of my bed and onto my knees, and I prayed to receive Christ as my Savior – and in that moment, everything in my life changed.

From the moment of my conversion through high school, Carl continued to play a prominent role in my life. Because I was unable to drive at that time, and lived in a spiritually disinterested home, Carl would drive 15 miles one way, three times a week, to pick me up (along with a host of other students) for church and Bible study. To this day, I marvel at his generosity to me and his commitment to the gospel. And yet, while I did not recognize it at the time, Carl took the opportunity to begin pouring the Jesus in him into me. To this day, many of the insights, disciplines, and knowledge I have of God were instilled into my life by those moments with Carl. He taught me how to walk with God through prayer and Bible study, how to share my faith, and how to teach God's truth to others. He challenged me in the areas of doctrine and apologetics – and maybe most importantly, he showed me how to distinguish the voice of God and think for myself in the Spirit. He taught me how to be a disciple and how to make disciples.

DISCIPLES MAKE DISCIPLES

After many years of slogging through the ministry of the local church in light of the commission of Christ to go and make disciples of all nations, I have come to the conclusion that too many well-intended believers, like myself, most likely have missed the boat. While many of us set sail on a course charted for Great Commission success, we have found ourselves marooned on an uncharted island of church and ministry ambiguity.

To be fair, this idea may not be palatable or even popular (sometimes the truth is hard to accept), but it is gut-level honest and necessary if we are to ever fulfill the commission our Savior left for us to accomplish. If I learned anything from Carl and his unorthodox way of ministry, it was that the church does not make disciples. Our pulpits and lecterns do not make disciples – and neither does the curriculum we peddle. While they often assist in the mission, no matter how determined and hopeful we might be to use such tools in making disciples, true disciples are made life-to-life through the investment of Jesus in us into another soul. Making disciples is always relational and organic in nature, and never institutional and organizational. All these organizational items can support the disciple-making process, but they in no way make disciples because *disciples make disciples*. Sadly though, we have made a mess of this truth. We have bought into the lie that our programs, parties, picnics, and practices make disciples; yet the evidence of our efforts shows otherwise. While at one time the four "B's" of babies, butts, buggies, and Bible may have gotten people onto church property (and those days are long gone), they never made disciples. Let us be honest, there is a big difference between being a kind-hearted, program-ized church-goer, and being a fully developing, reproducing follower of Jesus.

Making disciples requires one maturing believer willing to take personal responsibility for another soul to aid them in becoming intimate with God. Oswald Chambers explained that the call of every Christian is to be broken bread and poured out wine to other souls until they are able to feed on God for themselves.[2] Meaning, disciple-making requires personal life-to-life investment. It requires a willingness to get one's hands dirty for the sake of the gospel as we willingly stick our hands into the goop and muck of another person's life to influence them for Christ. As such, disciple-making requires personal, one-on-one investment and concern. It requires interaction, dialogue, accountability, and responsible mentoring. Why? Because this is God's plan. It has always been (and will always be) His plan. God requires that His people, as maturing followers of Christ, make disciples of others life-to-life – and this requires more than a church service and Sunday School class.

So, what are we to do? If we would take a moment to honestly assess the fruit of our ministries and the strategies we often employ, we would discover that for all our effort, at best, we have made

---

[2] Oswald Chambers, *My Utmost for His Highest*, (Grand Rapids: Discovery House, 1963), September 30.

Jesus-loving, inconsistent churchgoers and few, if any, disciples. Yes, this could seem blunt; but this does not mean it is untrue. All we have to do is investigate the fruit of people's lives. Are they truly intentionally living on mission for God? Are they seeking intimacy with the Father and then living in pursuit of His will for their lives? Are they willing and able to speak their faith and engage in relevant spiritual conversation? Do they hear from God regularly and respond in obedience to His calling? By all evidence, the answer appears to say – not as much as we might hope. Good churchgoers…, maybe; but intimate, reproducing followers of Jesus?

Who or what is to blame for this result? Ultimately, there are a plethora of contributors both spiritual and fleshly. So, rather than trying to narrow down who or what is to blame, maybe the best thing to do is just own our reality and begin moving in a new direction toward our commission. What is certain is that while unfortunate, in the average church setting, we are too busy trying to herd the masses and mobilize the ministries to be concerned with making disciples. After all, Sunday is coming and the show must go on; and do not forget that the next calendar event is coming soon too. Truth is, we are seemingly elated when people just show up for church or for the event we are hosting – and we are practically ecstatic when people volunteer to serve. This has caused us to call their participation "discipleship" as we move on with the program? But deep down, we know this is not Great Commission, but instead a fatal and foolish mistake.

If we are going to change course to realign with God's calling, it will require pastors to rediscover their primary calling to *equip the saints* (see Ephesians 4:11-13) instead of being eloquent pulpiteers and chaplains of compassion. It will require the church programs to truly become relational instead of organizational. It will require simplifying our ministries to allow for people to have time to engage in Great Commission living. If this is to change, it will require a paradigm shift in the thinking of *how* we do church and *why* we do church. It will require that we get our eyes back on the ball so we do not fumble away our opportunity for the Great Commission of *presenting everyone fully mature in Christ* (Colossians 1:28).

CHAPTER 2
THE JESUS WAY

The church changes the world not by making converts,
but by making disciples.
John Wesley

HAVE YOU EVER heard the phrase, "Rome wasn't built in a day?" It means that important, quality work takes time. Of course, if you have ever been to Rome or to places in the world where Roman culture was introduced, you would quickly come to appreciate this statement. Yet in our fast-paced, modern world, we live in an era of instant everything. Whether it is instant food, instant gratification, or instant success – we want it, and we want it now! Unfortunately, such a mentality has found its way into the church resulting in far too many church members and pastors expecting instant success in the form of an instant mega-church. But ministry and disciple-making do not work that way. The Great Commission is far more crockpot than microwave. It takes time. It requires intentionality. The Great Commission is won in the trenches of life far more than it is won on the platform through preaching. Disciples are made over coffee sharing life more than they are made by pastors preaching sermons.

Recently, I was dialoging with a younger, up-and-coming pastor, and what became apparent was his desire for quicker success than he was experiencing. He was seeking instant success and acknowledgement without having to put in the sweat and spiritual equity essential to making a dent. By all appearances, he was pursuing fanfare and more prestigious opportunities so that he could expand his options and move up the church ladder. But life and ministry do not work that way. In fact, if a minister is looking for instant success, they have chosen the wrong calling and profession. Sure, there will be a few quick success stories, but seldom do they last. Great Commission takes time, patient intentionality, and an outpouring of the Holy Spirit.

CONVERSION INVERSION

Over the past few years, in contemplating a number of questions surrounding the idea of making disciples and fulfilling the Great Commission, it appears that we are doing a number of things in Jesus' name, including making disciples, that have nothing to do with Jesus or His strategy for accomplishing His mission. Like the apostle Peter in the Garden of Gethsemane, we think we have been doing the right thing by taking matters into our own hands, not realizing our zealous activity in the flesh has been working against us and the commission of God. Coupled with burrowing deeper each day into a post-Christian culture where Christianity is no longer in vogue, the modern church is in rapid decline becoming at best impotent and at worst obsolete. To make matters more challenging, in too many instances, the church has become too rigid to adjust to relevancy or too compromised, unwittingly peddling Christ without commitment.

To complicate matters, instead of returning to Jesus' model of ministry, we have plunged deeper in neo-manmade methods following the next ministry fad to arrive on the scene. This appears to be an absolute re-defining of what it means to be Christian, and it more closely resembles cultural correctness than it does biblical alignment – and now, authentic followship has given way to a faith of comfort and convenience. Tod Bolsinger may be correct in saying that, "Christendom as a marker of society has clearly passed."[3]

---

[3] Tod Bolsinger, *Canoeing the Mountains*, (Downers Grove: InterVarsity Press, 2015), 12.

How is it that the church has seemingly lost her way? One of the reasons we have lost our way is because we have lost our understanding of why we exist and how we are to exist. Somewhere along the way, we lost sight of the calling to make disciples and thought our mission was to make converts and build churches. We have done neither well because only disciples, not converts, can build sustainable churches. Maybe Mike Breen was correct when he said, "If you make disciples, you always get the church. But if you make a church, you rarely get disciples."[4] We have so focused on church growth that we have lost our way and exchanged the mission of God for a lie of self-promotion. As such, with our well-intended attention turned to conversion and church buildings, we unintentionally dumbed down the idea of a disciple settling for something less than God's standard. Honestly, this was not intentional; but truthfully, it is easier to make a convert and churchgoer than it is to make a disciple; not to mention that conversions and baptisms are much easier to count.

What happened? It appears we exchanged Jesus' method for making disciples with our own ideas and concepts. In our zealous pursuit for instant success, we inverted Jesus' model of disciple-making and mistakenly embraced a conversion theology fixated on winning the lost through mass production. Instead of focusing on the individual, we prioritized ministry in bulk thinking we could make it up on the backside – and we have not. The idea has been, "If we can just get them on our property, into our programs, and have them listen to our pulpit, then they will accept Christ, get baptized, and become disciples." If only it was that instantaneous. Yet according to Jesus' example and calling, this is not how disciple-making works. Disciples are made one at a time and never in bulk. Certainly, converts can be wooed and entertained in bulk, but not disciples – they take time and intentionality. The result is the modern church, for whatever reason, has chosen a strategy of ministry that is exactly the opposite of the method Jesus modeled focusing on conversion over making

---

[4]   Mike Breen, *Building a Discipling Culture*, (Pawley Island: 3DMovements, 2011), 11.

disciples. Now, in a post-Christian culture, this strategy is being exposed for its flaws with faith abandonment, declining church participation, and cultural compromise.

WALK THIS WAY

In a cursory review of the gospels and Jesus' earthly interactions, we discover that He performed ministry to four primary groups (see chart below). Jesus engaged the masses, the seventy, the twelve, and the one. In each of these engagements, He met people at the point of their need to move them toward experiencing and moving into intimacy with God. But unlike our current church models, Jesus did not start with the masses, He started with the one. He was more focused on maturing the twelve than He was entertaining the seventy. Jesus started small and prioritized investing Himself in the few to impact the masses.

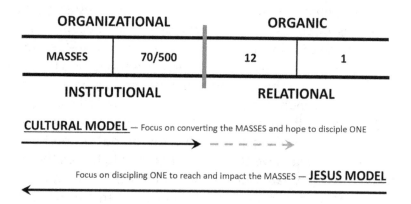

Without a doubt, Jesus had an impactful ministry to the masses. It is obvious from reading the gospels that Jesus seldom met a microphone He did not like. In fact, Jesus seldom if ever passed on an opportunity to speak to a crowd about the Kingdom of God and the Father's will; yet this was not His priority focus. Whether He was preaching the Sermon on the Mount or feeding the five thousand, while He might have been proclaiming the truth of God to the masses, if you look closely, He was doing all these things primarily for the benefit of mentoring the twelve men following Him. Jesus was preparing them for the moment that they would take up His mantle upon His departure. Certainly, while anyone present could have benefitted from listening and responding to Jesus, each one of these wonderful events and teachings were part of His investment into His disciples.

The second group of people Jesus influenced included those who followed Him from a distance. Referred to as the seventy up to the five hundred, Jesus had a regular input of instruction to this crowd of people who were interested in his teachings and activities, but who were not a part of the twelve disciples. Some might consider this group to be those who followed from a distance or when it was convenient, although many of them were present at some time after the resurrection (see 1 Corinthians 15:1-3). In either case, this group was not His priority either, although Jesus certainly made a personal investment of truth into them. In fact, He was constantly proclaiming "hard teachings" to sift this group to differentiate the true seekers from those who enjoyed following for the show. Nonetheless, Jesus seldom missed out on an opportunity to speak truth into this crowd as He saw them as sheep without a shepherd since many of the religious leaders had abandoned them for earthly gain.

The third group that Jesus shared His daily life with was the twelve disciples. A cursory reading of the gospels quickly reveals that this was the group of men of highest importance to Him. These men were Jesus' heartbeat. He shared life and poured all of Himself into them with the expectation that they would pour their lives into others. The relationship Jesus had with these men was absolutely organic and personal in nature. Everything He did with the masses and with the seventy was for the growth and benefit of the twelve. Jesus trained them and invested in them, because He knew one day, He was going to depart, send the Holy Spirit, and turn everything over to them.

Here is what we cannot miss. Unlike the church today, Jesus did not start with the masses or with the crowd, He started with the twelve. His ministry moved from the personal to the public, from the organic to the organizational, from the twelve to the masses – and not the other way around. Unfortunately, this is not how we have organized the church today. We are more focused on the masses than on the twelve. We have built our churches on programs and events to garner a crowd so that we might proclaim the truth in the hope of making a convert. We have placed our hopes in the creativity of the pulpit personality, rather than in the life-to-life investment of discipleship. While this sounds noble, it is the opposite of Jesus' example. The question is why? The bottom line is because it is easier. It is easier to preach from pulpits and teach from lecterns than it is to spend time with people one at a time. This is not to say that preaching has no place in the church – it does. We know that historically, since the inception of the early church, that God has used pastors and the pulpit to make a difference in people's lives. However, the pulpit can never substitute or become the primary tool for disciple-making. Unfortunately, it appears that we have mistakenly come to think that we can impact more people in a crowd than over a cup of coffee? Or can we? Also, it is much less messy. When we deal with people one at a time, it can get really messy; and who has the time, energy, and courage to stick their hands in the goop of people's lives? Answer... JESUS did! And this is what He taught His disciples to do. But so long as we preach from behind pulpits and design great evangelistic programs and events to reach converts to make them clean, we will not have to get our hands dirty making Jesus-following, Great Commission-centered disciples. After all, is this not what our curriculum and programs are supposed to accomplish? We cannot rely on some other resource to accomplish what Jesus asked us to do. If we truly desire to see the Great Commission accomplished, we cannot delegate it to someone or something else.

With this in mind, the time has come for us to abandon our flawed, faulty, and failing attempts to make converts and return to the method and strategy Jesus offered to His disciples. The good news is the Great Commission works in a pre-Christian, Christian, and post-Christian culture when we engage in it the way Jesus showed us. Will it take time and patient intentionality? Absolutely! More importantly, it will require the ministry of the

Holy Spirit to lead us. But as we shift from making converts to making disciples, we begin to see once again a great awakening in our land and around the world. Rome was not built in a day, and neither will disciples be made in a day either.

CHAPTER 3
LOSING JESUS AT CHURCH

The parents of Jesus lost Him at church,
and they were not the last ones to lose Him there.
Vance Havner

HAVE YOU EVER been hit in the head with a 2"x 4"? I am not talking literally, but spiritually. Has God ever so invaded your space, and turned your life upside-down to the point where you began to see things right-side-up? Several years ago, while serving my seminary internship at a church in Albuquerque, New Mexico, I was invited to speak at a retreat for college students in the hills outside of Santa Fe. Honestly, I had no business standing in front of anyone to speak on behalf of God because of the internal struggle I was experiencing in my faith. At that particular moment, I was spiritually exhausted and disgusted. Frustrated. To be frank, I was angry and disappointed with God and myself. As a result, I was questioning my desire to embrace God's call upon my life for ministry because I had become so disillusioned with church and the Christian life. I was running on fumes at the brink of burnout because I had lost Jesus at church among all of the programs, events, and expectations. The result was I had a gross spiritual inferiority complex because in spite of going to church, reading my Bible, praying, giving, and going to visitation, I felt like I was failing at being a Christian. While I was busy at religion, I was bothered by the emptiness I was feeling being a "good Christian."

It was my own fault. In my ambition to serve God and find my path for ministry, I found myself caught up in the program of the church and focused on fulfilling the expectations of other people – and I lost Jesus. I lost the intimacy I once held dear that was instilled in me through my spiritual mentor – Carl. I had lost the passion to know the Savior I was striving to serve. I had lost my focus on the priority of making disciples in exchange for keeping the program of the church running smoothly. Honestly, after only a few years in the "ministry," I felt as if I had become the Program Director on the Love Boat instead of a disciple maker living out the adventure of the Great Commission.

Not coincidently, but in perfect step with God's will and timing, an interesting thing happened to me one evening after our general session. As I was heading back to my cabin, I stumbled across an opportunity to learn how to Two-Step. Loitering in front of the cafeteria at a Baptist encampment, I noticed a group of college students up to *no-Baptist* good. Being the inquisitive sort (and single), I thought I would take a peek, just to make sure my supervision was not needed. Much to my surprise, some cowboy from Texas Tech University had provoked a Baptist flash mob with the stereo in his pick-up truck – inciting a raging foot-function at a Baptist encampment. Humored by the scenario, I took my two left feet to the party and joined in the fun. Of course, there was one small problem; I did not have a clue how to 'Two-Step.' So, after thoughtful and careful consideration, I approached an attractive young co-ed (who I thought could become my future wife) and invited her to teach me how to dance – and she mercifully agreed.

Thankfully, this young lady had the patience of Job. After providing me with a verbal explanation of the finer points of the "Two-Step," she whisked me off to the asphalt dance floor to test my ability to apprehend her instructions. There we were, cheek to cheek, arm and arm, my toes trampling her toes as I gazed at my feet, all the while muttering under my breath the count of "1-2-1-2-1". Then it happened. After several missteps and miscues, I felt a gentle nudge within my conscience as God cut in on my dance. The next thing I remember was this sweet, young lady jerking my chin up from my downward gaze and asking, "Are you dancing with me or are you dancing with your feet?" In that moment, God pierced my life unlike ever before. There in the hills outside of Santa Fe, God pulled me close and forever altered the trajectory of my walk with Him by hitting me with a spiritual 2"x4" upside my soul.

Now, I realize I cannot speak for others, but for several years, I had been under the impression that God was only pleased with me if I was doing the "Christian" thing and doing it well. My spiritual condition was measured by my intensity in the disciplines of the faith. I was caught in a vice of constantly trying to please and impress God by making others believe I was a better follower of Jesus than what I truly was – and the result was, I had become spiritually disappointed. While I did not realize it at the time, I was so busy trying to fulfill the rules and regulations of a modern-day Pharisees that I did not recognize that on the inside I was tired, empty, and craving for something more. I had been duped into believing the Christian life was about performing the disciplines of the faith and making converts; and thus, I was a busy Christian, but not necessarily a fulfilled and joyful follower of Jesus.

So, in the moment that I was arm in arm, cheek to cheek, and face to face with God – the immediate result was a faith-quake from which I have yet to recover. I had a God encounter in which God gently whispered in my ears, "Joey, you've been dancing, but not with Me! You've been trained in the steps of the spiritual dance, and yet you have seemingly missed the point of the faith dance. As a result, instead of experiencing intimacy with the Author of your faith and the Lord of the dance, you have succumbed to a religious experience instead of a Divine expression." Yes, I had lost Jesus at church – and all in the pursuit of ministry. I had surrendered intimacy and maturity for performance and applause – and I had not even realized it. But then God, on that unforgettable evening, showed up to invite me to take my eyes off of the things of earth and church, so that I might look deep into His wonderful face to enjoy the Spirit dance.

However, that was not the end of the lessons. After apologizing to the young lady, I took my eyes off my feet and fixed them onto her, and an amazing thing happened – my feet started to do what was correct. In just a few minutes, I went from stepping on toes to twinkle-toes. As we began to laugh and twirl, dip and stomp, you might of thought that you were watching the country music version of Fred Astaire. What I have discovered is that in the process of having God step on my toes, that if we will take our eyes off our feet and the steps of the Christian life, and look fully into God's wonderful face, that our spiritual lives will begin to work too. When we fix our eyes on Jesus and lose ourselves in the pursuit of enjoying intimacy with the Father, the dance can be enjoyed and it will come supernaturally. Yet whenever we focus on the steps rather than the Savior, we will always miss the warm embrace of the Master.

SETTLING FOR LESS

How is it I lost Jesus at church and why have so many others seemingly lost Him there too? Truthfully, there are many answers. We can be certain that some of the reasons are personal and self-inflicted, but not all. Likewise, we can be sure that some are due to the well-intended, man-made schemes of the church gone awry. Sadly though, in our zeal to reach the world and grow the church, we have broken away from Jesus' model and commission in exchange for a way that seems right to ourselves – and the result is we have built a church that is responsible for creating a *Frankenstein* faith. Instead of being a Great Commission, organic, life-changing community, we have become an organization fix-ated on human goals and achievement – and Jesus' commission has become a program to be run rather than a relationship to be shared.

Our dilemma begins with a subtle yet devastating confusion of terms. Along the way, we have incidentally confused a *convert* for a *disciple*. In fact, in many instances, we are using these terms inter-changeably, but they are not one in the same. A convert is not necessarily a disciple, but to be a disciple you must first be a convert. In fact, let me go ahead and set the record straight on this matter. In the Great Commission in Matthew 28:19-20, Jesus issued one command. It was not to *go*. It was not to *bap-tize* or *teach*. It was to *make* disciples. The only verb in the Great Commission is *matheteuo* – which means *make disciples*. The other three words are participles explaining what a disciple is to do – which is to *go, baptize,* and *teach.*[5]

Needless to say, understanding this word is critical to knowing Christ and living out the Great Commission because Jesus' commission is not about conversion and then discipleship – it is about a genuine belief marked by obedient followship. Thus, baptizing and teaching are not separate jobs to be performed (like they are so often taught in most of our churches), but necessary aspects to help a person to genuinely know and follow Jesus.

With this truth there is some good news and some tough news. The good news is Jesus was crystal clear in His choice of words about what a disciple is. The tough news is, it is not what many people have made it today. In our world of easy believism and conversion theology, we have accidentally peddled a definition of "Christian" that is less than God's expectation. If the word for disciple (*matheteuo*) refers to one who trusts and obeys, then it is speaking of a person who believes in and follows Jesus as they put into practice the faith they profess. This means a disciple is more than a convert – and more than a person who goes to church, prays a prayer, walks an aisle, gets dunked, takes communion, and then lives however they want to live independently of God. A disciple is a person who so genuinely believes Jesus was who He said He was, and did what He said He did, that they trust Christ as their Savior and Lord, and abandon themselves to live obediently on mission with Him. This is what Jesus had in mind in John 8:31-32:

> To the Jews who had believed him, Jesus said, "If you obey my teaching, you are really my disciples. Then you will know the truth, and the truth will set you free."

Jesus' point is simple – obedience to God's Word and mission is the only true evidence of belief. It also means Jesus cannot be

---

[5] John MacArthur, The MacArthur New Testament Commentary – Matthew 24-28, (Chicago: The Moody Bible Institute, 1989) 341.

your Savior without also being your Lord, because to be a disciple requires faith that results in action, belief that leads to obedience, and trust that results in followship. Anything less is no faith at all.

In returning to how the church got into this precarious position, it is important to recognize that there was no mischievous intent here. What has happened in our desire to win the world for Christ is we have placed a higher premium on evangelism than we have on true followship, and the result is a cheapened grace that affords a mentality of *Christ without commitment* or surrender – which is no salvation at all. Likewise, we have built our church models and programs around this same evangelistic strategy and then created a scorecard that measures our human success at accomplishing our missional objective. The only problem with such a disposition is that we have had to lie to ourselves about the reality of the state of our churches and denominations while the evidence of a declining church and its impact is staring us in the face. Even more, we think the solution is to create and publish yet another evangelism strategy like it is a magic pill to solve all of our ills and failures. By the way, we do not have an evangelism problem, we have an intimacy and loving God problem – because people always talk about the things they love and are most intimate. The issue is followship and not witnessing.

The simple reality is God never intended for His church to be so eternally-minded that we abandon the necessity of earthly relationships and interaction for the sake of the gospel. If we learn nothing from Jesus' encounters with the Pharisees, first and foremost, the gospel must be personal if it is ever to have a life-changing impact; otherwise, it will be relegated to producing well-intended, religious pretenders who see life and ministry as some religious exercise enjoyed in a cul-de-sac of human effort or lack thereof. So, what can we do to turn the tide?

FROM GOOD TO GOD

A few years ago, as I was wrestling with my own convictions and sense of expectation as a pastor, God birthed in my heart an understanding of *why.* At first, I fought with God, and like a spoiled little child, I put my hands over my spiritual ears in the hope and anticipation that I could block out His convictions – only it did not work. Patiently, God kept speaking into my life to confront my false and misappropriated ministry assumptions to redirect my heart back to His Word and will. Trust me when I tell you, I did not go down without a fight. I struggled deeply, primarily, because what was going on inside of me felt so contrary to most of my ministry education and the voices in church culture – and certainly contrary to my church experiences. Whenever I would dialogue with friends in the ministry, most of them would look at me as if they were hearing Greek for the first time since seminary. Furthermore, it fell far outside the expectations placed on me by the churches I served and the education I endured in preparation of my calling to become a pastor. Nonetheless, as I became more and more honest with myself, and the condition of the people I had been called to pastor, I began to soften and become more attentive to the Spirit's leading. Simultaneously, God began to stir ideas in my mind to begin leading me into a new direction – back to His Word and in sync with His commission, all the while creating in me a thirst and desire for more.

It all began to ramp up one evening in Gainesville, Georgia when I was asked to teach a group of lay leaders the book of Colossians. As I began preparing to work expositionally through Colossians, immediately, I was overwhelmed by Paul's intercessory prayer in chapter 1.

> For this reason, since the day we heard about you, we have not stopped praying for you. We continually ask God to fill you with the knowledge of his will through all the wisdom and understanding that the Spirit gives, so that you may live a life worthy of the Lord and please him in every way: bearing fruit in every good work, growing in the knowledge of God, being strengthened with all power according to his glorious might so that you may have great endurance and patience, and giving joyful thanks to the Father, who has

qualified you to share in the inheritance of his holy
people in the kingdom of light. Colossians 1:9-12

Okay, confession time! As many times as I have read and
studied this Prison Epistle, I had never truly taken the time to
consider what Paul was praying. Yet before any of you cast shame
upon me for this miss, my guess is you too have breezed over
these verses like you would roll through a stop sign on an abandoned country road. But let me tell you, this prayer is packed with
critical spiritual truth worthy of our time and understanding. In
fact, when I finally stopped and took the time to dive deeper into
Paul's words, God began a new work in my life.

Before we dive into this prayer, may I first introduce a critical
thought? If we were to poll the average church member or person
in our community about what it means to be a *good* Christian
(what it means to be a disciple), we would most often hear results
like – a good Christian goes to church, reads their Bible, attends
a small group, is moral, and they usually give, pray, and serve.
While each of these answers is noble and possible, and might
even sound correct, they do not fall into agreement with what
Paul prayed for the Colossians (see chart below).

GOOD Faith	GOD Faith
Go to Church	Filled with God's Will
Read Bible	Bearing Fruit
Pray	Growing in Knowledge
Mission Trips	Strengthened with Power
Serve/Help Others	Having Endurance
Moral/Kind	Showing Patience
Spiritual	Grateful in Spirit

Upon closer inspection, we discover that Paul's list includes not one of the items we might use to qualify another person's faith. Quite to the contrary, his list is vastly different. In this prayer to the believers at Colossae, he intercedes to ask that the Colossians would be *filled* (*pleroo*), a passive verb in the Greek, to capacity by an outside source (the Holy Spirit) so that they might walk in a manner worthy of the Lord to please Him in every way. Which is to say, Paul prayed they would walk with Jesus under the influence of the Holy Spirit in such a manner it would put a smile on God's face. Much like a person under the influence of a foreign substance, Paul prayed the Colossians would be intoxicated and directed by the Holy Spirit in all things dwelling under the influence of God. This reminds me of Paul's words in Ephesians 5:18, "Do not be drunk with wine, but be filled by the Spirit." Then, in the subsequent verses, Paul continues on to describe the various elements which signal a life that is truly pleasing to God.

Instead of championing a list of good religious activities that any person can manufacture in their flesh through their human abilities and ingenuity, Paul prayed they would experience and live in the disciplines of the faith that can only be produced by the work of the Holy Spirit abiding within them living through them. So, in Colossians 1:9-12, he prayed they would *bear fruit in every good work, grow in their experiential knowledge of God*, that *they would be strengthened in their sense of patience with people and with circumstances*, and that *they would always give thanks to the Father for His goodness and faithfulness to them.* Paul prayed for something completely different than what we have been told to do and to pursue in the modern church. He prayed for the movement of the Holy Spirit while we have been content to pursue God in our human ability and ingenuity.

A quick exegesis of the details of Paul's prayer reveals amazing insight into a Holy Spirit-led life. Paul's prayer suggested that a life whose objective is to please God is a life well spent and that the single-minded ambition of any Jesus-follower is to think and act only on those things that satisfy the heart of God. Thus, Paul seemingly concludes that a life that puts a smile on God's face is in sync with the Holy Spirit and His will. Such a life will always produce five essential elements.

PLEASING TO GOD

First and foremost, a God-pleasing life is always producing the fruit of the Spirit. Now, to produce such fruit, an individual must have an authentic union with Christ through salvation and then dwell under the influence of the Holy Spirit on a daily basis, because it is impossible to produce the fruit of the Spirit independent of the Holy Spirit. Jesus spoke of this in John 15:5 in what is known as the "abiding" life. He said, "I am the vine and you are the branches; if any man abides in me and I in him, he will bear much fruit; but apart from Me, you can do nothing." Spiritual fruit includes any Godly quality that buds in a person's life because of Christ in them; and then as the Holy Spirit works in them, their lives bloom into behavior generated by the Holy Spirit that honors God and points others to Jesus.

The second trait of a God-faith is a Holy Spirit-led maturing intimacy with God. When Paul prayed growing in the knowledge of God, he was speaking of experiencing a continuous action of maturing by coming into full awareness and understanding of who God is and what He has called His followers to do. This is both qualitative and quantitative. It is information leading to transformation and inspiration – we *know* God so we *show* God! Furthermore, it is quite empirical in nature, meaning that God is being physically, intellectually, emotionally, and socially experienced in tangible ways, even though the Christian life is spiritual in nature and driven by faith. God is so real to me that it seems like I am experiencing Him empirically.

In praying that the Colossians would be strengthened with power, Paul was speaking of an explosive reoccurring power that propels a believer toward a stronger more fervent faith. Like spark plugs and pistons continually firing inside of an engine to propel the vehicle forward, the Christian life is propelled forward by a God-inspired internal explosion. In other words, God is allowing and authoring experiences in our lives to draw us closer to Him

23

and to allow our lives to intersect with the lives of others so that His will can be accomplished in and through us. The result of this leading is that we grow in endurance and patience. James speaks to this idea in James 1:3 when he said, "Consider it joy whenever you encounter trials of many kinds because you know the testing of your faith produces endurance."

When the Bible speaks of endurance, it is most often referring to learning how to have patience in any circumstances. The Greek term refers to having the ability to see things through under great distress. It refers to a person who will not become frustrated with their circumstances because they understand that God is moving and working to ensure that they are in proper alignment with Him. Often, God allows trials and testings in our lives because we have fallen out of alignment with Him, choosing a way or disposition that seems right to ourselves. So, He uses these circumstances to bring us back into alignment with Him so that we will again live under His influence. Because He loves us and desires that we strive in intimacy with Him, He affords these opportunities because He wants us to trust Him with all of our heart and mind instead of leaning on our own understanding, abilities, and ingenuity (Proverbs 3:5-6). So, when we fall out of alignment, to get us into the correct position under Him so that we might acknowledge Him and put Him first in our lives, He uses circumstances to direct our steps.[6]

Sometimes He uses circumstances, while at other times, He uses people. The term for *patience* refers to being longsuffering with people. It is a reference to how we treat other people. Paul is praying that under God, we would have the ability to treat others the way Jesus would treat us even though they are treating us the way they treated Jesus. Chew on that idea for a moment. Can I treat others the way Jesus treats me when others treat me the way they treated Jesus independently of the Holy Spirit? Absolutely not! Loving others with an agape love is only possible through the Holy Spirit.

---

[6] Information found at www.preceptaustin.org.

The final quality Paul prayed for the Colossians was a true sense of gratefulness. Simply stated, the Holy Spirit within us is always thankful for the presence and power of God in our lives no matter our struggles or circumstances, because we know God is present, for us, and will never leave or forsake us.

DO YOU SEE WHAT I SEE?

What exactly is the ultimate difference between these two lists? The "good" list is what we can manufacture in our own ability and through our own efforts; while the list that Paul prayed can only come as a result of the work of the Holy Spirit in and through a person living in absolute submission to God. The "good" list is what many people consider to be acceptable Christian behavior today, and yet it has nothing to do with biblical followship. Sadly, our current list of acceptable religious experience is manufactured in God's name, while Paul's list is the result of a surrendered, Spirit-led life. In other words, for far too many professing Christians, they are living the Christian life in their ability rather than under the influence and direction of the Holy Spirit – and such a life is less than God's heart and desire for His followers.

Why is this significant? Because what is being promoted and taught through many church ministries today does not align with God's will and heart for His church. Furthermore, it is regrettable that we have come to believe that in our noble attempt to reach the world, we may have embraced a model of ministry that has worked against our commission to make disciples all in the name of making converts. The result is we have redefined what a disciple is and settled for a manmade "good" faith instead of a Spirit-led "God" faith. To make matters worse, we have established an entire means of ministry that supports this undoing as we have settled for a strategy opposite of Jesus' example – and the result has been profound. Quite frankly, we have settled for making converts even though our commission is to make disciples when they are not one and the same! We have settled for dancing with our feet instead of dancing with our Lord.

25

Maybe the time has come for us to take our eyes off of our feet and our well-intended ministry schemes, and lift them to the One whose name is above every name. Maybe the time has come for us to stop worrying about what others think, say, and do, and return to the example Christ has set for us so that maybe, just maybe, we can return to the joy of our salvation with a willing Spirit to sustain us. Maybe, just maybe, if we will look deeply into the eyes of our Savior, and seek first His kingdom and righteousness, then our feet will start doing what is right and we will enjoy the dance of authentic, intimate faith.

CHAPTER 4

ABIDING CLARITY

*The fruit of the Spirit is the outward evidence
of the inward reality of a heart abiding in Christ.*
Richard Foster

MAY I ASK a sensible, yet poignant spiritual question? It is not a question you have likely ever asked yourself, but it is a critical question to ask and answer. Can a person bear the fruit of the Spirit independently of the Holy Spirit? Furthermore, can a believer live the Christian life without the guiding influence of the Holy Spirit?

Before you answer this question, let me encourage you to think deeply into passages like Galatians 5, Colossians 3, and Philippians 4. For while we might think we have the ability, and even the responsibility, to live the Christian life in our *good* flesh, in actuality, it is impossible to live the Christian life without our complete surrender to the Holy Spirit. So, can a person live the Christian life and bear the fruit of the Spirit independently of Holy Spirit? Absolutely not! Never! But this in no way keeps us from trying. In fact, we are all pretty good at living in the flesh and manufacturing a good, religious lifestyle. At least, I know I am a wily veteran at this endeavor.

I must confess that I spent years trying to convince myself the Christian life was Joey doing his spiritual best to please God rather than Joey allowing the Holy Spirit to lead me as I surrendered my will for His will. I wrestled with the reality of John 15:1-5 and the abiding life. I understood the concept, but struggled to live under the influence of the Holy Spirit. This changed one Sunday morning while teaching on the fruit of the Spirit in Galatians 5. In the midst of explaining the gospel and its impact upon our lives, off the cuff, I drew up a diagram on the white board that has become a primary tool for assisting people in identifying where they are in their journey of faith.

LOST			FOUND	
REBELLIOUS	**RELIGIOUS**	**S A L V A T I O N**	**FLESH-LED**	**SPIRIT-LED**
A person who has not trusted Christ and who lives in rebellion towards God unconcerned about their faith	**S P I R I T U A L** — A person who believes in God but trusts in their religion or good works instead of in Jesus for salvation		A person who has trusted Christ as Savior but attempts to live the Christian Life in their own abilities and goodness	**S U R R E N D E R** — A person who has trusted Christ as Savior and lives under the influence of the Holy Spirit bearing the fruit of the Spirit

The premise of the diagram is that there are only two types of people in this world – those who are *lost* and those who have been *found*. Those who do not know Christ as their personal Lord and Savior, and those who do. What determines lost from found is salvation. That is, when a person is introduced to the love of God expressed in the life, death, burial, and resurrection of Jesus, that person experiences the invitation of grace through the wooing conviction of the Holy Spirit, and then by faith, they believe and receive God's grace and mercy. It is only in receiving God's grace through faith that a person is moved from death to life, into a relationship with God, and into citizenship in God's Kingdom. This reality is clearly expressed in Colossians 1:13-14:

> For He has rescued us from the dominion of
> darkness and brought us into the kingdom of
> the Son He loves, in whom we have redemption
> through His blood, the forgiveness of sins.

In this passage, Paul explained that through our response to God's grace and mercy, He rescues us from sin and then colonizes us into His Kingdom by adopting us as His children through the finished, atoning work of Christ on the cross.

To appreciate our need when we were lost, we also need to understand there are two kinds of lost people – those who are *rebellious* and those who are *religious*. Jesus spoke of these two types of people in Luke 15 in the parable of the Prodigal Son.

If you are unfamiliar with the parable, Jesus is confronting a group of Pharisees about lostness and who is in need God's grace. He offered them this thoughtful parable to confront the reality of their actual faith condition. It is interesting that while people often focus on the younger brother in the parable, the parable was actually more about the older brother than the younger brother – as they were both prodigals. The younger brother represents the *rebellious* lost that included everyone who was not a teacher of the Law or a religious Pharisee. He represents the common man who is both aware and unaware of God who regularly chooses a way that seems right to himself.

In recounting the parable, the younger brother goes to his father and asked for his inheritance, basically telling the father that he wished his dad was dead so that he could get what was coming to him. Little did he know what was really coming to him. Nonetheless, he took his inheritance, went and squandered it in wild living, only to find himself eating leftovers with the local swine population. To put it bluntly, he hit rock bottom – which was not kosher (pun intended). Eventually, he came to his senses, got up, and went home, where his father was waiting with arms opened wide to be reconciled with his lost son. It is a beautiful picture of God's grace and our need for repentance.

On the other hand, back on the family farm was the older, pious brother who was quite unhappy that his father was so willing to receive his younger brother with such grace and mercy. If we were speaking King James, you might say that he was *ticketh off*. Of course, the older brother represents the *religious* lost – and this was Jesus' real audience. Jesus was calling out the Pharisees and religious establishment who were so close to the Father yet so far from the truth. In this parable, Jesus was confronting these men for their misguided and misappropriated faith that saw themselves as more spiritual, and more redeemable, than the common person of society. Instead of actually caring for God's people as God intended, they had gotten on their spiritual high horses and had abandoned their spiritual duty. This is why Jesus often said the common people of Israel were *sheep without shepherds*.

The Parable of the Prodigal Son teaches us that it does not matter whether a person is rebellious or religious, they are still lost and in need of a Savior. In fact, Jesus inferred to the Pharisees that it is more likely for the rebellious lost person to find God than it is for the religious lost to find Him because they actually see their need for God through the harsh reality of their lostness. Nonetheless, both are in need of the cross to change their eternity.

On the other side of salvation and the cross are the *found*. The *found* are those people who genuinely have received Christ as their Lord and Savior, and who have been rescued from their lostness by the generous grace and mercy of God. Like the lost, the found also includes two kinds of people – those who are saved and living the Christian life in their flesh (flesh-led), and those who walk under the influence of the Holy Spirit in an abiding life whose lives produce the fruit of the Spirit (Spirit-led).

After years pursuing Christ and serving in the ministry of the local church, I can confidently say without hesitation that the vast majority of Christians live the Christian life under their power instead of plugged into the power of God. We have been conditioned to attempt to please God through our own abilities, ingenuity, and effort. Not only does it come naturally to our flesh patterns, it often gets supported through misguided and misunderstood teachings. We have become conditioned to strive to do our spiritual best, in the hopes of pleasing God with our adjusted good behavior. This is where I found myself so many years ago. I was saved, but I only knew how to manufacture my faith instead of living in an abiding intimacy with God – and I was miserably unfulfilled and disappointed.

Referring back to the Good Christian/God Christian diagram in the previous chapter, the flesh-led Christian life is nothing more than an attempt to do good enough to earn God's favor and blessings. But the Christian life is not first about doing; it is primarily about being. As James 3 discusses, *our works do not produce our faith, rather our faith produces our efforts*. Therefore, when we know who we are and whose we are, we can serve God out of the overflow of our intimacy with Him. Yet so long as we attribute intimacy with behavior, we are going to struggle. Why? Because the Christian life is more than a life trying, but failing to please God through our goodness. Can you imagine how miserable the Christian faith would be if our salvation was contingent on our goodness instead of God's grace? I can – and I did! A life that is pleasing to God is a life that knows Christ as Savior and then lives under the influence of the Holy Spirit in an abiding life that produces the fruit of the Spirit. Anything less is to change the scorecard God has established in His Word to identify true faith and followship.

Sadly, not only have we found ourselves irreconcilably frustrated within our souls knowing something is amiss within us, the church has reinforced this unfortunate, yet well-intended mis-teaching. Far too many pastors, church leaders, and Sunday school teachers know how to walk more comfortably in their good flesh than in the Spirit, and have taught people how to walk in their good flesh too. Furthermore, we have changed the scorecard to fit our spiritual narrative so that we can feel better about our spiritual impotency, although I am not so sure we recognize our challenge. Instead of measuring our success by transformed, Jesus-following, disciple reproducing, Holy Spirit-driven lives, we have defined spiritual success by our morality, church attendance, and participation to church activities. The result is we have not denied ourselves, taken up our crosses, and followed Jesus as we were instructed in Luke 9:23-26.

Like it or not, the Spirit-led life is God's intended plan for everyone who has called upon the name of the Lord for salvation. Biblical Christianity is not only a life that has come face to face with grace and by faith has received Christ as Savior, it is a life that has determined to live submitted to the influence of the Holy Spirit allowing Jesus to be our Lord, Master, and Boss. The Christian life is a life surrendered to the will of God, the Word of God, and the abiding presence of the Holy Spirit. This is the life God desires and has made possible for His followers, and anything less, is less than God's best. Lest we forget, our faith walk cannot be obtained through our abilities and efforts, but only through God's ability and power living in and through us. This is a daily, moment-by-moment endeavor requiring our constant trust in God and obedience to His leading and Word. It is a life that certainly requires our engagement, responsiveness, even our culpability, and it cannot be lived apart from the Holy Spirit. God does not want us to settle for less than His best; He desires that we *know Him in the power of His resurrection and in the fellowship of His suffering* – that we might be conformed to His person.

CHAPTER 5
RETHINKING CHURCH

It's not so much that the church has a mission, it's that the mission of God has a church.
Alan Hirsch

CHURCH. WHAT DO you think when you hear the term? I think of the child's limerick – "Here's the church, here's the steeple, open the door and see all the people." More importantly, what is the purpose of the church? If you asked a hundred random people, you are likely to hear few answers that are the same. For me, based on Acts 2:42-47, the church is a gathering of believers in Jesus, who have abandoned themselves to honor God as they live on mission to make disciples of all nations.

It goes without saying there is no such thing as a perfect church because churches are filled with imperfect people. Every ministry within every church is flawed for this same reason; yet this does not mean the church is antiquated, irrelevant, or unimportant. Nor does it mean the mission of the church has been lost. Quite to the contrary, any church with the right mission and focus can be relevant for kingdom purposes. Unfortunately, based on declining numbers, pressure to conform to political correctness, a rapidly changing culture, pervasive carnality in the lives of people, and compromised, flesh-inspired teaching from far too many pulpits and lecterns, the number of churches with a true gospel-focus appears to be dwindling fast.

THE MISSION OF THE CHURCH

In the past thirty years, there has been a definitive influx of business principles thrust upon the church challenging local congregations to define their missional purpose for existence. As a huge proponent of taking a church through this process, I am thankful that church after church has rightly applied many of these leadership principles to bring clarity to their congregants. Even entire denominations have sought to employ these principles in hopes of bringing forth a Great Commission reformation. Most often, it all begins with asking the question – what is God's mission for His church?

Re-discovering the mission of the church is a relatively easy question to answer. According to Scripture, the mission is to make disciples of all nations and to present everyone fully mature in Christ (see Matthew 28:19-20 and Colossians 1:28). This includes the church gathered and the church scattered. Collectively and individually, the priority of the church is to share the message of God's love, grow in His love, and continually repeat the process with others.

This moves us to the next logical question – what is a disciple? Until we define and qualify this objective, no church or ministry can intentionally participate in the Great Commission. In defining a disciple through Scripture, I have concluded a disciple is an abandoned follower of Jesus who participates in the mission of Christ to make disciples of all nations. A disciple is someone who knows the Lord, seeks to please the Lord, and engages the world in Jesus' name. Ironically, we toss the term *disciple* around so casually, yet when we ask professing Christians to define it, they often cannot. One thing is certain, a disciple is much more than a convert, and the Great Commission is more than evangelism.

CONVERT VERSUS DISCIPLE

Among many churches and leaders today, the terms *convert* and *professing believer* have become substitute terms for *disciple* – yet these are not the same. While conversion is an essential element to being a disciple, it is NOT the only thing. As discussed earlier, a disciple is someone who believes and obeys and not someone who believes and then obeys. This is not semantics. The Greek term, *matheteuo*, requires belief and obedience. Thus, a disciple is one who is so convinced of the work of Christ, they trust and follow. They surrender their will for God's will. Their spiritual default has been switched from off to on, and they now live to fulfill God's calling on their life. Yes, there is growth and maturity in the process, but there is also authentic abandonment which leads to direct obedience. The end result is that there is a difference between being a convert and being a disciple, between professing faith and actually following Jesus.

There is no intent to diminish the necessity of conversion in the process of salvation; rather, the intent is to raise the bar back to God's standard to minimize the cheapening of grace. Bonhoeffer offered a thoughtful discourse on this idea in *The Cost of Discipleship*:

> Such grace is costly because it calls us to follow, and it is grace because it calls us to follow Jesus Christ. It is costly because it costs a man his life, and it is grace because it gives a man the only true life. It is costly because it condemns sin, and grace because it justifies the sinner. Above all, it is costly because it cost God the life of his Son: 'Ye were bought at a price', and what has cost God much cannot be cheap for us.[7]

For this reason, Jesus was clear in his choice of terms – a disciple trusts and obeys. There is no true conversion without obedience and followship. So, for the scores of people who profess Christ and get baptized in our churches, yet their lives never reveal change or result in following in obedience to Christ's commission, there is reason to question the authenticity of their

---

[7] Dietrich Bonhoeffer, *The Cost of Discipleship*, (Munich: Christian Kaiser Verlag, 1937), 45.

profession. Consider 2 Corinthians 5:17, "If a person is truly in Christ, the old is gone and all things have become new." Paul was explaining that unless conversion results in obedient followship, then there is good reason to believe that true conversion never actually took place.

In diving deeper into this concept, we see that a true Jesus-following disciple not only follows, they *make* too. A disciple is a disciple maker and *alongsider*. To walk in the way of the alongsider, a Jesus-follower begins taking personal responsibility for another soul to move them into intimacy and surrender with God. While there is no one path to making a disciple, there is a clear destination – Jesus! Ultimately, a disciple looks and acts like Jesus. Thus, when a man or woman has reached that place where their spiritual default switch has been flipped from *me* to *Thee,* then we are beginning to get somewhere in the world of true discipleship.

The paradox of the Great Commission is that it is to be accomplished both individually and collectively. Yes, disciples make disciples, but the church is also called to make disciples. This was Paul's encouragement to the Colossians:

> He is the one we proclaim, admonishing and teaching everyone with all wisdom, so that we might present everyone fully mature in Christ. Colossians 1:28

By all appearances, because many churches have bought into making converts instead of making disciples, the church has struggled to make disciples. In prayerfully considering the state of the church, the question of how have we gotten to this place needs to be asked. How has the ministry become defined by our personalities, activities, and programs instead of by the true development of the people we have been mandated to shepherd? Where is the commission to make disciples in the midst of our parties and programs? It would appear that many churches have had to redefine the mission to keep the program alive, because the strategy will never accomplish Jesus' mission.

THE MODEL CHURCH

Several years ago, in prayerfully investigating the various church models in existence, a simple diagram came to mind that helps to determine a church's focus. The premise of this quadrant model is that ministry is built upon two crucial priorities – *relationships* and *missional responsibility*. That is, churches focus on people and a God-ordained purpose. Each of these priorities has a sliding scale from high to low. Thus, every church finds its identity and strategy in the tension between a drive for purpose and a genuine and intentional focus on people.

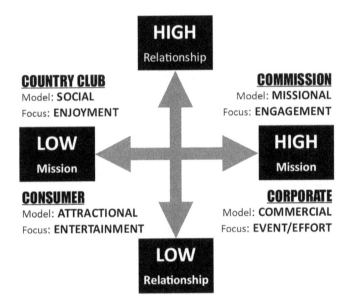

A church's identity and focus can be plotted with an honest assessment of these priorities of relationship and missional responsibilities. The more a church leans in a particular area, the more it shapes that churches values and determines its model. For example, a church with a high relational value and a low missional expectation will look very different from a church with a low relational value and a high missional expectation, even though they both would say they are Great Commission churches. Likewise, of the different models, each church has its strengths and weaknesses; and no one style is necessarily better than the next – just different. There is an exception though. It is my personal conviction that only one style of church actually has the ability to accomplish Jesus' mandate of making disciples – the Commission (Missional) Church, that is focused on a high relationship and high missional responsibility ideology. Organizationally, each of the others can only hope to make converts.

THE COUNTRY CLUB CHURCH

What do you get when a group of people gather together who enjoy spending time with one another, who genuinely care for each other, but who have a small or insignificant missional purpose – that is, a high relationship/low mission culture? Time and again, whenever I have posed this question, the answer has been the same – you get a *Country Club* environment!

A church built on a high relationship/low responsibility model tends to become a spiritual country club where the focus is on meeting the needs of the congregation instead of actually accomplishing the Great Commission of making disciples of all nations. This church often places a premium on the social relational aspects of congregational life while unintentionally minimizing the priority of Jesus' commission. Thus, this kind of church tends to focus inwardly at the expense of putting on blinders with regard to the world around them – and any conversion that might take place most likely comes from the individuals within the church. The tendency of this church is to be less intentional on reaching people and making disciples while all the systems of the church are geared to maintaining peace and offering community within the programs and events offered. This kind of church accomplishes this priority by addressing the comforts and conveniences the membership desires.

The reason this church struggles to make disciples is because the ministry is about the programs and keeping the people content. Of course, this does not mean the church is ineffective or irrelevant. Such a church can be highly effective in making converts among church members, but unless there is a primary disciple maker within the body investing Jesus in them into others, this church will find itself focused on keeping the masses happy and occupied for the kingdom.

THE CORPORATE CHURCH

Moving diagonally across the chart, the question becomes, what do you get when you find yourself in a high responsibility, low relational environment? This is where the mission comes before the people, and everything that is done is driven by meeting goals and objectives established by the leadership. I call this the *Corporate* model.

In the corporate model, the church tends to run like a business where the pastor is often viewed as the CEO and the driving force of the organization. During the heyday of the *Church Growth Movement*, this model of church often served as a flagship church within its community setting the standard of ministry many other churches attempted to follow. Generally speaking, the environment was pastor-driven, vision heavy, program-based, and event-centric – all for the purpose of sharing the gospel and winning the world. While this might sound correct, there have been a couple of unfortunate side effects – conversion focus and burn out! Evangelism, and not disciple-making, is the mantra of this style of church at the expense of orphaning converts after spiritual birth and leaving them to discover for themselves how to live the Christian life. Even more, this type of church is set up and driven to make converts instead of disciples, these baptized believer's default to living flesh-led spiritual lives because the message and missional strategy of the church is not set up to expect obedient followship or to nurse people to spiritual maturity. At best these churches rely on curriculum to grow these converts to maturity; yet curriculum can only offer them information and not transformation. Why? Because *disciples make disciples!*

This compromise leads then to a different struggle – burn out! Burn out becomes a pervasive issue in this style of church because of the massive number of staff and volunteers required to keep the ministry churning and the lack of focus on discovering the joy of salvation in intimacy with God. Thus, while these churches might be incredibly evangelistic, reporting a number of converts and baptisms, this church model wears people down and burns them out with little to no relief. Church members feel used and abused. They often become disillusioned, because they discover over time that in spite of genuinely wanting to serve God, they have been serving the egos and agendas of men. People might be busy for the sake of the kingdom; they are also exhausted possessing little spiritual bandwidth. Such a strategy of ministry also perpetuates a false sense of ministry and Great Commission, leaving most people confounded and frustrated with little sense of true spiritual fulfillment.

THE CONSUMER CHURCH

Moving to the bottom left of the diagram, introduces us to an entirely different beast. What do we find in a setting where there is a low relational component and a low commitment expectation? Before you jump to conclusions and say the dead church, you might be surprised to discover the fastest growing church in America – the *Consumer* church. This is a church that puts on a great show and is usually centered around a charismatic and effective public speaker. This church often has all the bells-and-whistles and does everything with excellence, yet unfortunately, it also has a very low commitment expectation of its attenders. More often than not, while this style of church has a prolific impact on drawing the unchurched, de-churched, and people frustrated in the *Country Club* and *Corporate* church models, it often offers these groups a chance to run and hide from genuine spiritual commitment. Furthermore, because this model tends to be highly attractional in nature, it also tends to prioritize ministry to the masses over ministry to the individual – resulting in a strategy of ministry that focuses on the main event of the worship service only. Over and over, as these churches have been attended and studied, this style of church appears to promote a ministry strategy that incidentally or intentionally peddles Christ with minimal to no commitment.

Here is the point, it does not matter if you attend or pastor a *Country Club* church, a *Corporate* church, or a *Consumer* church, these are all well-intended churches who have decided to do church in a certain, cultural manner that is *convert*-focused. One style focuses internally, the other pushes externally, while the third wants to give people enough to stay connected while not expecting too much so as to pressure people into following Jesus. But make no mistake, in each of these churches, there is a true desire to minister to people, to see people come to Christ, and to help people to experience a good, healthy life. Still, we are fooling ourselves if we think any of these churches are intentionally making genuine disciples of Jesus. The reason they cannot is because they are not organized to accomplish such a feat. In each of these church styles, disciples are not being made because of the church's intentionality and strategic planning is counter-productive to making disciples. Yet, if by chance disciple-making is occurring, it is because there are individuals within the church who are working outside of the church strategy (and often against the plan of the church) to make disciples. Quite simply, conversion driven churches, because of a masses-ministry agenda, are not designed to make disciples. They can help people check a religious box and feel good about themselves; however, they are not releasing the church into a Great Commission, disciple-making ministry. It is a flawed design. These churches often peddle a good faith that people can manufacture through their own abilities instead of a God faith that can only be produced by surrender to the Holy Spirit.

THE GREAT COMMISSION CHURCH

Which brings us to the top right corner of the diagram – the *Commission* church. This is the only type of church capable of actually making disciples because this church model prioritizes and balances relationship with spiritual responsibility. Such churches do not make conversion the finish line, they make it the starting-line.

In fact, the driving force of the ministry is to prioritize interpersonal relationships to help people experience true intimacy and expectancy with God. Of course, this is not near as easy as it sounds.

The Commission church is a ministry that equally values relationships and missional responsibility. It is a ministry that prioritizes people over programs, intimacy with God over religious conjecture, fosters biblical koinonia over casual community, and God's truth over cultural correctness – such a ministry is capable of making disciples. It is an atmosphere that emphasizes dialogue over monologue and prioritizes one-to-one and smaller group relationships over large assembly instruction absent from an opportunity for discussion. This is not to minimize the proclamation of truth from pulpits and lecterns, it is to prioritize interaction. If the gospel is anything, it is relational both with God and with others, always requiring discourse.

Paul underscored this concept when he wrote to encourage Timothy and Titus. In 2 Timothy 2:2, Paul clearly instructed Timothy to take the truths Paul personally had invested into him, and re-invest these truths into reliable men who will be qualified to teach others. Such a process obviously requires relationship and conversation. In no way was Paul encouraging a "sit still and instill" approach to ministry, rather a ministry strategy identical to the approach modeled by Christ with the twelve. Without a doubt, Jesus was the master at introducing truth and leading others to embrace and understand it through directed conversation and questioning. How often did He share a parable or object lesson and then wait for his followers to engage with Him in dialogue to embrace its meaning?

In Titus 2, Paul continues this idea as he encouraged Titus to foster a culture of *laleo*. While the term is a bit ambiguous, many scholars believe Paul was charging Titus to create an environment of dialogue where faith is discussed and not just passed down. In Titus 3, one could even argue the value of men discipling men and women discipling women. This discipling concept is based on the idea that truth is caught more than it is taught and that the more we wrestle with truth in discussion, the more we are likely to apprehend it and not just comprehend it.

The ramifications for such an approach to ministry seeks to create interaction at all levels. For example, whether it begins with a sermon, a bible study, a quiet time, or a spiritual conversation over a cup of coffee, opportunities for dialogue and questioning led by a maturing disciple, and coupled with accountability, will afford a genuine chance for spiritual investment and growth. In such an intentional approach, there is more than follow up, there is follow through. People tend to live out what they understand and grasp. Likewise, the more people share in community, the more they can fulfill the idea of iron sharpening iron.

In pondering this idea, I was inspired to create a new approach to encourage the members of my church to unite in their daily pursuit of Christ. The concept was simple, create a devotional pathway that chronologically follows in the footsteps of Jesus throughout His earthly ministry to learn alongside of the twelve what it really means to follow Jesus. The idea was to challenge people to strap on their sandals to become the thirteenth disciple. Only, they were to do this with one to eight other people, to learn together and from each other as they journeyed together. The results have been remarkable. As people have disciplined themselves to daily engage in a systematic Bible reading plan of the life and ministry of Jesus and then come together to share and discuss their revelations, it has proven to be monumental in developing spiritual muscle and fortitude. Likewise, it has fostered authentic community. Such an approach is just one of many strategies that can promote a proactive Great Commission climate within the local church.

A WORD OF ENCOURAGEMENT

Before we go any further, a word of encouragement would be appropriate. Discipleship and disciple-making are not easy. Making disciples is challenging and costly. The reason is simple, like water, human nature is often to take the path of least resistance. Furthermore, making disciples is challenging because it is difficult and dirty work – and most people have neither the time nor energy to get their hands dirty. It is much more convenient, and certainly less threatening, to make church-goers from pulpits and lecterns than it is jump into the trenches of Great Commission ministry and find yourself waist deep in humanity. Face it, people are messy! They are time consuming! It is much easier to plan an event and teach a lesson than it is to do life with another soul. After all, who really has time for making disciples? Yet this is our commission. We are called to go into the world and make disciples of all nations – and this will never occur if we are not willing to get a little dirty for the sake of the gospel.

Making disciples can be challenging because people are difficult. People are often obstinate, opinionated, and disliking of change. Discipleship requires change! People never seem to get Jesus *like I do*. They have this uncanny ability to fall away and chase after things that lead them astray – whether it is into rebellion away from God like the prodigal son, or into religious activity that reflects the heart and behavior of the older brother.

Which brings us back to the mission of the church. Far too many people have lost Jesus at church because of how we have come to do church and because of what we have been teaching and how we teach it. In our expedient, consumer-driven culture, we have settled for tickling ears to gain attendance and offering attractional creativity without expecting surrendered commitment. The result is we have promoted and settled for a good faith instead of seeking a God faith.

In Colossians 1:28, we find a powerful statement of purpose espoused by the Apostle Paul to the believers at Colossae. He contended the mission of the church was to proclaim Christ by instruction and admonishment *so that we might present every person fully mature in Christ*. In other words, our mission as a gathering of believers is not to make converts who are orphaned at spiritual birth, but to see people from conversion to disciple-making maturity in Christ. To do this requires that we do more than teach people how to be good, but rather how to be Godly. This is not an easy task in light of the patterns and practices we have established in our churches where we have often established a ministry strategy that proliferates the good at the expense of God.

CHAPTER 6
FOLLOW ME!

God created the world from nothing; so long as we are nothing,
He can make something out of us too.
Martin Luther

MOST OF US are familiar with the child's game, *Follow the Leader*. In the game, whatever the leader commands and performs, everyone else has to follow suit. Several years ago, while suffering for Jesus and serving with the International Mission Board in Europe, I was invited to lead a ski retreat for students in Austria. Yes! It was a dirty job, but someone had to do it. One day on the slopes, we decided to play *Follow the Leader* on skis. Here is how it worked: The leader took off down the slope of his choice, whether a beginner, intermediate, or an advance slope, and everyone else had to follow the path and perform the moves the leader made. If he skied backwards, then everyone else had to ski backwards. If he hit a jump, then those following also had to hit the same jump. Well, as fate would have it, on one particular run, I was number two in line behind a crazy Canadian named Patrick – who just so happened to be a hotdog skier. Of course, Patrick chose an advanced mogul run. As he started down the slope, zipping through the moguls, all of a sudden, he popped a perfect helicopter jump (a 360-degree spinning turn). Being second in line, I set my skis downhill and headed to my demise. The next thing I remember was some German man standing over of me saying, *"Alter, das musste weh tun!"* which translated means – "Dude, that had to hurt?" And it did!

Following someone else is not always easy. Have you ever tried to follow someone in rush hour traffic in Atlanta? It is near impossible! The same is true as it pertains to following Jesus – it is not always easy, yet it is required.

Regarding following Jesus, in Matthew 4:19, Jesus invited the four amigos Peter, Andrew, James, and John, to follow Him so that He could make them fishers of men. Basically, Jesus invited them to go wherever He went, to say whatever He taught them to say, and to do whatever He modeled for them to do. In following in His footsteps, Jesus promised them He would make them what He needed them to become for the sake of the gospel. Yet the focus of Jesus was not just on them becoming fishers of men, it was also on their decision to drop their nets to follow Him. Until they surrendered to His request and let go, the door to following Jesus remained closed, but once they dropped their nets, Jesus could do something wonderful in and through their lives.

To appreciate this calling requires that we understand what it means to be a disciple. The term **disciple** refers to a student or apprentice – one who follows and patterns their life after their teacher. In Jesus's day, a disciple was a student who followed and learned from his rabbi. Wherever the rabbi went, his disciples went. Whatever the rabbi taught, his disciples learned and retaught. Whatever the rabbi did, his disciples did too. A disciple, quite literally, followed in the footsteps of his rabbi.

A BRIEF HISTORY

Ray Vander Laan, in his study entitled, *In the Dust of the Rabbi*, provides some fascinating insight regarding what it means to be a disciple. In Jesus' day, a rabbi was a spiritual teacher and influential leader – and the rock star of his day. He was known for pouring His life and convictions into his disciples to help them to know and serve God. Most young boys aspired to follow in the footsteps of a rabbi as his *talmidim* (disciple). So, should the opportunity arise, a boy would leave everything to follow His rabbi.

Around the age of five or six, a Jewish boy would begin his education at the local synagogue. In *Bet Sefer*, the child would memorize the first five books of the Old Testament (the Torah) – that is, Genesis through Deuteronomy. Upon completion of Bet Sefer, most boys went back to their family business to begin apprenticing, but if a young man was considered the best of the best, he would be invited to continue his education participating in *Bet Midrash.* In Bet Midrash *(house of study),* the student would learn the rest of the Hebrew Scriptures and the oral tradition including the Torah, Talmud, and Mishnah! This process occurred between the ages of 12 to 15.

On completing Bet Midrash, the exceptional student had the option of returning home or applying for *Bet Talmid* to become the disciple of a rabbi. In this step, the young man would go to his local rabbi where he would be quizzed on his knowledge of the Torah, Talmud and oral traditions. If the rabbi thought the young man met the standard of followship, he would invite him to "come follow me." If he did not think the teen was the best of the best of the best, he would encourage the young man and send him on his way. Of course, for the young man he called out, he would leave everything behind to follow and serve under his rabbi for the next several years. In this process, the *talmidim* would learn his rabbi's yoke – that is, this particular rabbi's teachings and interpretation of the Law and traditions. Upon successful completion of this internship, the young man would become a rabbi.

Tradition holds that whenever a rabbi came into a town with his entourage of disciples, all lined up in a pecking order of tenure and excellence, the people would line the streets to show their appreciation for the rabbi and his disciples. During this time, a saying emerged among the wisemen and sages, "May the dust of your rabbi fall upon you!" That is, may what your rabbi is teaching you stick! We hope and pray you get it so that you can effectively minister and lead all of us.[8]

Enter Jesus. When Jesus called out to a band of fishermen to come and follow Him to be His disciples, He was extending a call to a group of young men who were not the best of the best (they

---

8   Ray Vander Laan, "Rabbi and Talmidim", www.thattheworldmayknow.com, 2021.

were in the workforce instead of in school), they were representatives of the common man. Yet His calling still required total abandonment as they had to drop the nets, their livelihood, and all that was familiar to them, to follow the Savior. It cost them everything to follow the Master.

THE COST OF DISCIPLESHIP

One of my favorite writers is Dietrich Bonhoeffer. Bonhoeffer was a German theologian remembered for his stance against Hitler and the Nazis regime and for his passion for authentic discipleship. While his book, *The Cost of Discipleship*, might be his most acclaimed works on following Christ, it is his writing, *Christ the Center*, that he made his most important statement on following Jesus.

> When a man encounters Jesus, He must do one of two things: Either he must die, or he must put Christ to death.[9]

This is one of those statements you can ponder seemingly forever to either wade in the shallows or drown in its immensity. Whether in reference to salvation or to one's daily followship, each of us has to come face-to-face with Jesus and His calling on our lives to deny ourselves if we are to ever seek first His kingdom and righteousness.

Jesus had this in mind the time He was with His disciples in northern Galilee at Caesarea Philippi. You might remember this moment from Luke 9. Jesus was with the twelve and asked them, "Who do the crowds say that I am?" Peter correctly responded, "You are the Christ!" This might appear on the surface to be a small event, yet to fully appreciate the story, we need to understand the setting. Caesarea Philippi was a Roman resort housing a number of religious shrines for people to pay homage to any and

---

[9] Dietrich Bonhoeffer, *Christ the Center*, (Munich: Christian Kaiser Verlag, 1960), 9.

every god known to the Romans. So, when Jesus poses the question, He was laying down the gauntlet for their followship. He was confronting the conviction of His disciples to affirm their faith and to teach them what is required to truly follow Him. Notice Luke 9:23-25:

> Then Jesus said, "If anyone would come after me (follow me), he must deny himself and take up his cross daily and follow me. For whoever wants to save his life will lose it, but whoever loses his life for me will save it. What good is it for a man to gain the whole world, and yet lose or forfeit his very self?

We read in this passage the three necessary actions every person is required to make if they are going to follow Jesus. First, they have to *deny* themselves – that is, they have to give up! Jesus told the twelve, if you truly want to follow Me, you have to make a voluntary act of surrender by denying your will for my will. You have to forfeit your personal desires and ambitions for a cause greater than yourself. In effect, it means that following Jesus requires waving the white flag of surrender realizing that He must increase and we must decrease (see John 3:30).

What must we surrender? We must surrender our plans for His plan and our kingdom for His kingdom. Instead of fixing our eyes on our priorities, we place them on Jesus and His priorities! Thus, following Jesus requires that we relinquish anything that inhibits us from following Him. It might be a personal ambition, a bad attitude, a denominational allegiance, or an unforgiving spirit. Yet, no matter what it is, our lives will never count for God until we surrender our will for His will and trust Him with all of our heart.

Next, Jesus told the twelve that to follow Him it would require they *take up their cross daily.* This is a direct reference to picking up and dragging a horizontal beam to a shameful death. Talk about an exciting proposition! No thanks! Yet, before we go running in the opposite direction, it might be helpful to understand that Jesus was not asking us to carry His cross, but our cross. After all, we are not capable of carrying His cross, but we can carry a cross that God uses to point others to the cross He carried for all of mankind.

Several years ago, my mother-in-law sent me a story regarding this idea. Apparently, a man at the end of his rope prayed, "Lord, I can't go on. My cross is too heavy to bear." God replied to him, "If you can't bear it, give it to me, and go and pick out a new one." Filled with relief, the man thanked God, and entered a room where he saw crosses of various sizes – some taller than skyscrapers and others as small as a dime. After searching for hours, the man spotted a tiny cross on a table he was sure he could bear. He said to God, "God, I'd like this one." God chuckled, "But son, that's the cross you just gave me." The simple truth is we all will have crosses to carry, and it does not matter the size of your cross. What matters is how you carry whatever cross God asks you to bear. Your cross will be anything you must bear to bring glory to God. It is any blessing or difficulty you must carry to reveal to others the cross of Christ.

Ultimately, after denying ourselves and carrying our cross, we also have to follow the teachings and example of Jesus. We have to get up and get going. The phrase, "and follow me," is an invitation to get in the game and put ourselves in a position for God to work in and through our lives by bringing your life into alignment under His Word and His will. It is learning to trust God and follow His leading in our lives. It is not living under the notion, "God, I'm going to do this, will you bless it?" but under His influence asking, "God, whatever you want me to do, I'll do it!"

What does this mean? It means there is more to being a disciple of Jesus than just following the crowd and attending church. It means a disciple is one who has counted the cost and is abandoned to following and living out the life and teachings of Christ to impact the world around them. It assumes that Jesus and His purposes are the motivating compulsion of one's life. It infers that the art of making disciples is not an organizational or institutional task, it is the task of every believer abandoned to the propagation of the gospel to the nations. The mission is not the church *gathered* but the church *scattered* that makes disciples. Of course, this in no way devalues the importance of the corporate church; it shifts the responsibility from the organization to the individual for the making of disciples. Returning us once again to the truth that disciples are made by disciples and not by pulpits and lecterns.

THE MARKS OF A TRUE DISCIPLE

After three and a half years of following in the footsteps of Jesus as His disciples, learning everything God wanted them to know and experience, in Matthew 28:16-20, Jesus extended His final call to His disciples that remains today as the primary qualifier of followship. In this passage, Jesus did more than extend the Great Commission, He laid out five traits of a genuine follower to help us see what is required to walk in His footsteps and to live this thing called the abiding, Christian life.

> Then the eleven disciples went to Galilee, to the mountain where Jesus had told them to go. When they saw him, they worshiped him; but some doubted. Then Jesus came to them and said, "All authority in heaven and on earth has been given to me. Therefore, go and make disciples of all nations, baptizing them in the name of the Father and of the Son and of the Holy Spirit, and teaching them to obey everything I have commanded you. And surely, I am with you always, to the very end of the age." Matthew 28:16-20

While the remainder of this writing is committed to diving deeper into these characteristics, it will be helpful to identify them and prime the pump for what is to come.

First, in verse 16, we see that disciples make themselves available to God because they have become absolutely convinced that Jesus was who He said He was and that He did what He said He would do. Thus, a true disciple shows up when God calls.

The second quality of a disciple involves worship, "When they saw Him, they worshiped Him." A disciple is someone who possesses a genuine affection and love for God that results in becoming a living sacrifice, holy and pleasing to God.

The third mark of a true Jesus-follower is they live under the influence of God's authority plugged into the power of God in an abiding life. They do not strive to operate in their ability and ingenuity; they operate in God's ability and power.

Next, a disciple lives abandoned to the agenda of God by *going into the world to make disciples of all nations*. While we know this as the Great Commission, it is actually just one of the five marks of a disciple – and that is, a disciple lives daily on mission to make disciples.

Finally, a disciple waits on the assurance of God to lead. The promise of God's presence is to go before us, to walk beside us, and to always stand with us as we pursue His heart and will. A disciple is one who knows Christ, tunes His spiritual ears to God's voice and leading, and then obeys God's leading.

CHAPTER 7
AVAILABLE TO GOD

The greatest ability of a Christian is his availability.
James Merritt

ONE FRIDAY EVENING as a freshman in high school, I was invited to dress out for the varsity football team. Now before you get too impressed, I was not the only freshman invited to practice with the team, attend the sacred pre-game meal, and put on the red-on-red monochromatic uniform. Furthermore, our varsity team was terrible, so it was as much a death wish as it was an honor. Nonetheless, I thought I was big stuff playing on the varsity team under the Friday night lights.

Now in the history of football at Cross Keys High School, I doubt any freshman had ever actually played in a game under the lights; but I was determined to change that legacy. Throughout the week in practice, I worked diligently to prove to the coaches I was capable of playing. But like Dan "Rudy" Ruettiger for Notre Dame, I was high on hopes, big in heart, yet lacking the size and experience to play. Nonetheless, I pressed on – and I had a plan.

Shortly after kick-off, it started to become obvious that I was not registering on the depth chart and my night of fame and glory was to be nothing more than modeling the uniform on the catwalk of the sidelines. So, I decided the time had arrived for me to spring my plan into action. The plan was simple. I determined the best possible chance I had to play would require that the coach would not just know my name, he would also know my whereabouts throughout the game. So, while my friends were on the bench picking splinters and guarding the water-bucket, I positioned myself right next to the coach, and no matter where he marched up and down the sideline, I was not going to leave his side. I was resolved he was going to know I was available and ready to get into the game. And my plan worked. After three quarters of play, and chasing the coach for what seemed to be miles along the sideline, either out of fatigue of looking at me or bumping into me, He called my name. Yes, while my buddies were sanding the old wooden benches with their backsides, the coach put me into the game! All 138 pounds soaking wet was in the game – and it was awesome. I made myself available to play – and I got into the game.

GO TELL IT ON THE MOUNTAIN

In Matthew 28:16, we find the first major characteristic of a follower of Christ is they are *available* to God. Matthew recounted, "The disciples went to Galilee, to the mountain where Jesus had told them to go..." The first mark of a disciple of Jesus is that he or she listens and responds to the leading of God, making themselves available to Him. They show up whenever and wherever the Savior calls.

To appreciate this verse, we need a little context. The region of Galilee is found in the northern portion of Israel encompassing the area just south of the Sea of Galilee (known as lower Galilee) and extending some forty-five miles north to the headwaters of the Jordan River at Mount Hermon (known as upper Galilee). Jerusalem was some eighty miles as the crow flies south and just east of Galilee, requiring a five to seven-day journey by way of Jericho.

In considering the timeline after the crucifixion and resurrection, most scholars believe this event likely took place some fifteen to twenty days after the resurrection. The question that piques my interest is on which mountain did Jesus invite the eleven to meet Him? Tradition holds it was Mount Arbel, which rises some seven hundred feet to overlook the Sea of Galilee. This would be a logical place for Jesus to give the Great Commission since the western road of the Via Maris ran alongside of Mount Arbel providing the opportunity for travelers to carry the news of Jesus throughout the known world.

Yet after several visits to Israel, and a time of personal study, I cannot help think that the mountain where Jesus met with the eleven and a few others, was on Mount Hermon in upper Galilee some forty-five miles north. This is the same area where many scholars believe the transfiguration took place and where Jesus asked his disciples, "Who do the crowds say that I am?" If this was the case, it reveals an even greater effort on behalf of the disciples to make themselves available to Jesus. Not only would they have to trek up Israel's highest peak from which they could see the nations around them, their commitment to following would also underscore the magnitude of their belief in the resurrection. Would you travel an additional forty-five miles and hike a 9,000-plus foot mountain to meet Jesus if you were not convinced of His resurrection and deity?

Also, by leaving Jerusalem after the resurrection and returning to Galilee to meet Jesus on the Sea of Galilee for Peter's restoration – and then returning to Mount Hermon, the eleven and a few others would have had to walk past nearly all of Jesus' teachings throughout their 3½ years of following in His footsteps. Furthermore, after receiving the Great Commission, they would have had to walk back to Jerusalem, past the majority of Jesus' ministry, taking time to reflect on all of Jesus' teachings in light of this commission.

Suffice to say, in either case, the effort put forth to make themselves available to Jesus speaks volumes of their belief and commitment to surrender their lives to Christ. Which brings us back to the first mark of a disciple. The first mark of a disciple of Christ is that they *listen, respond* and *show up* to God's leading because they are available to God.

ABSOLUTELY CONVINCED

I have a confession. I am not a huge fan of revivals and crusades. While I have many friends in evangelism who I admire for their faithfulness, I have never been a big fan of corralling my friends for a pizza dinner and show to attempt to convince them to receive Jesus. This does not mean revivals and crusades cannot be effective, it just is not my preferred way of sharing the gospel. Nonetheless, I do remember a moment at a revival I attended in my early twenties where the speaker made a statement that has since been tattooed on my soul. In speaking about one's belief in Jesus as Savior, and in the certainty of having received Jesus as one's Savior, the evangelist asked, "Do you know that you know that you know?" I interpreted his question to mean, are you absolutely convinced Jesus was who He said He was and that He did what He said He would do?

In reflecting again on Matthew 28:16, it is important to acknowledge that after the crucifixion and resurrection, the eleven disciples did not have to go to the mountain; yet something compelled them. Something motivated them to make themselves available to Him. As a result, when Jesus called, they did not hesitate to respond. My hunch is that once you have put your fingers into the nailed-scarred hands of a man raised from the dead, it has a profound effect on your willingness to respond to his request. When you become convinced of the reality of Jesus' purpose to seek and to save the lost, and you have come face to face with resurrected grace, it tends to have a big influence on your life. I am reminded of Paul's words in 2 Corinthians 5:14-15:

> For Christ's love compels us, because we are convinced that one died for all, and therefore all died. And he died for all, that those who live should no longer live for themselves but for him who died for them and was raised again.

Paul explained that as believers, like the disciples, we should be compelled by our absolute conviction that Jesus is who He claimed to be (God in the flesh) and that He did what He said He would do – die on the cross and rise from the dead to make a full atoning sacrifice for our sin. We should be compelled because we are convinced of who He is and what He has done.

We become available to God when we put ourselves in a position for God to work in and through our lives. We do this by uploading His Word into our minds, while we strive to remove the obstacles, issues, and ambitions that inhibit Him from having complete access to us. Meaning, it does not matter how talented, gifted, wealthy, or smart a person might be – if we have not made ourselves available to be used for His purposes, then we will be useless to God. Even while all of us acquire, cultivate, and demonstrate great abilities, as it pertains to God, there is only one ability that is the greatest ability of all. It is not our sociability, compatibility, accountability, adaptability, ingenuity, or reliability? The greatest ability is our availability. If we are not available to God, it does not matter what other abilities we might possess. Why? Because ability without availability is always a liability.

LIVING PASSWORD PROTECTED

To be available means we place ourselves totally, absolutely, and completely at God's disposal for Him to do anything and everything He wants to do in us, through us, with us, for us, and oftentimes, in spite of us whenever and however He chooses. Anything less would be to put restrictions on God. It would be to write a self-serving exclusion in the fine print of our commitment contract to Christ. For no one will make themselves available to God so long as they are concerned and consumed with their own comfort and conveniences. This is the challenge we face in following Jesus, especially as American Christians trying to alleviate the tension between biblical Christianity and our cultural religion that is being influenced by the American dream. We have to wrestle with the decision of whether or not we are going to live out our life mission and ambition or His life-giving mission and will? Will we say, *"Wherever He leads I'll go,"* or *"God, I'll go... if you send me to where I want to go and to the life I want to live."* Ultimately, we have to decide how much access we are going to give to God.

It reminds me of a problem my wife and I had to deal with when we gave our children cell phones for the first time. Upon handing them their phones, we clearly explained that the phones belonged to us and that we were allowing them to use them. We also explained that they were not to go to places on these phones they knew we would neither go nor approve – and that if we ever wanted access, they had to give it to us. Of course, what happened was, the first time we wanted access to their phones, they did not want us to know their passwords. So, quick, fast, and in a hurry, we had to have a *come to Jesus* meeting about the phones. It went something like this: "Make the phone available and accessible to us NOW – or lose the phone!" The problem was, they wanted all the rights and benefits to the phone, but they did not want the accountability and responsibility that came with it.

In like manner, we will never develop a willing and available heart for God until we know genuine humility and dependence on God. Likewise, if we attempt to live our spiritual lives *password protected* refusing to give God access to our hearts, we will miss out on His will and plan for our lives. Yet, when we make ourselves *available* to Him, we release God to move in and through us *exceedingly abundantly more than we can ask or imagine* (see Ephesians 3:20).

Consider Isaiah. In Isaiah 6, Isaiah had a close encounter with God where his life was shattered by the glory of God. He saw himself in light of who God is, and his response was, *"Woe is me. I am undone."* He got a glimpse of the holiness of God and could only respond saying, "God, I am nothing and I need you." So, God sent an angel to extend grace to him, and upon experiencing God's forgiveness, He heard God call, *"Who will go for Me?"* And Isaiah said, *"Me! Me! Me! Here I am Lord, send me."* Why? It was because of the amazing, life-transforming work of God in his life. His only reasonable response was to make himself available to God.

Such is true of each of the men and women in God's *Hall of Faith* in Hebrews 11. A cursory look into their lives reveals that not one of them had any great quality or skill about them. Not one of them was worthy or deserving of God's favor over their lives. In fact, in every instance, they each lacked the necessary skill to accomplish God's work and will; yet because of faith applied, when everyone around them was drifting, these faith heroes made themselves available to God because they were convinced God was true and that His way was better than their way.

Faithful followship does not begin with knowing where we will be serving the Lord or in what capacity. It does not start with having a clear calling to a certain ministry, occupation, or even in a definitive direction. It begins when we make ourselves available to God by surrendering our will for His will and as we set aside all reservations and preconceptions to go all in with Jesus. Let me say it another way, God can use no one greatly for His will and work, for His glory, until they willingly make themselves available to Him by abandoning themselves to His will in their lives. This cannot occur until, like when I was in ninth grade playing football, we put ourselves in a position to allow God to put us into the game. But when a person makes themselves available, it opens the door to the greatest adventure known to man – the Great Commission, Christian life. I appreciate the way Chambers said it, "If you give God the right to yourself, He will make a holy experiment out of you – and God's experiments always succeed."[10]

---

[10] Oswald Chambers, *My Utmost for His Highest*, (Grand Rapids: Discovery House, 1963), June 13.

CHAPTER 8
AFFECTION FOR GOD

Every heart has a throne and every throne has a God or god.
Who or what is sitting on the throne of your life?

SEVERAL YEARS AGO, I stumbled across an insightful video by the drama group, OneTimeBlind, entitled, *The Stool*. In this poignant, yet humorous video, a young lady is wanting to give God control over her life by giving Him His rightful seat on the throne of her life – only it was not as easy as she had hoped. The clip begins with Kat saying, "Jesus, I have decided to give you this..." (handing Jesus the stool). Jesus responds, "Really? Kat, you know whomever sits here makes all the decisions?" Kat replies, "I know, Jesus, but Your decisions are perfect, so giving this to you is my last decision!" (and Jesus sits on the stool). It is from here that things begin to unravel fast!

Kat is faced with a number of situations where she can choose her way or God's way – where she can resist or submit. Before you know it, Kat has pushed Jesus off the stool and she is now holding it – hoping to give it back to Him. Jesus then asks Kat if she is going to sit on the stool or if He is going to sit on the stool. Kat responds by saying, "I didn't know this was going to be so hard!" Jesus then says, "Make a choice." Kat replies, "I can't!" And the clip ends with Jesus saying, "You just did!"[11]

Talk about stepping on toes. This video pulls no punches and speaks directly into what is one of the greatest issues in life – who

---

[11] Information found at www.onetimeblind.com.

is going to be in charge in you? Who is going to sit on the throne of your life? Who is going to lead and who is going to follow? It speaks to the heart of worship and having an abandoned affection for God.

EVERY HEART HAS A THRONE

Whether we know it or not, every heart has a throne and every throne has a God or god – the big, hairy question is who or what is sitting on the throne of your heart? God has designed all of us with an internal throne where He wants to sit, although we do not always allow Him to sit there. This is the heart of the first Commandment, "You shall have no other gods before me." It is also the heart of a fully developing disciple of Jesus. Yet until we settle this issue of who is sitting on the throne within us, we are going to struggle with following Jesus as His disciple.

In Matthew 28:17, Matthew reported that when the disciples reached the summit of the mountain where Jesus asked them to meet Him, and they saw Him, *"they worshiped Him!"* That is, they loved Him with all of their heart, mind, soul, and strength – and gave Him access to every part of their lives. This act speaks to the second quality or mark of a true Jesus-follower – and that is, a disciple has *affection* for God. If we are disciples of Jesus, then we will be an affectionate worshiper of Him. It means we have given Him the rightful seat on the throne of our heart because we love Him with all of our heart, mind, soul, and strength. He is truly the object of our affection.

To appreciate this truth requires a little context. When the disciples met Jesus on the mountain top, much had transpired in those fifteen to twenty days after the resurrection. Jesus had introduced Himself to the men on the road to Emmaus and to the disciples in Jerusalem. The disciples had traveled back to Galilee to resume their fishing careers. Jesus had already forgiven and restored Peter on the shores of the Sea of Galilee. Then, somewhere in this time, Jesus asked the remaining eleven disciples (minus Judas), and a few other followers, to meet Him on the mountain. So, either at Mount Arbel in *lower* Galilee or Mount

Hermon in *upper* Galilee, they assembled to meet with Jesus — some for the first time since the resurrection (this is the reason some doubted). Some present had only heard the news of the resurrection but had yet to lay eyes on the Savior. With this in mind, take a moment to re-read the passage:

> The disciples went to Galilee to the mountain where Jesus had told them to go. When they saw Him, they worshiped Him; but some doubted... vs. 16-17

Did you see it? They all showed up and when they saw Jesus, they began to worship Him unlike ever before!

Can I tell you what did not happen? When they saw Him, they did not break out in song, preach a sermon, take an offering, and call it worship. They did not get in a circle around Jesus, hold hands, and sing, *Kumbaya*. They did not do anything that we do in our churches today to satisfy their preferences and then call it worship. They did not make it about themselves. No, in that moment, as an act of genuine affection and worship, they loved Jesus with every fiber of their being for who He was and for what He had done for them — and their worship was all about Jesus and honoring Him.

THE HEART OF WORSHIP

It is worth noting that the Greek term for worship used in this passage is *proskuneo*. The prefix *pros*, means *before;* and the heart of the word, *kuneo,* means *to kiss or adore.* This compound word carries the idea of making an offering or giving a kiss toward someone out of utmost respect, awe, and reverence for who they are.

In ancient Persia and in the Middle East, the kissing gesture was offered as a salutation. Interestingly, when two people were of equal authority, they would kiss on the lips. When there was a slight difference in influence or position, they would kiss on the cheek. But when one party was inferior to the other, the inferior party would prostrate themselves on the ground to kiss towards their superior – this is the idea here. The disciples worshiped Jesus based on the fact of who He was and what He had done.[12]

In this instance, the disciples and other followers present, fully recognized and embraced Jesus for who He was and what He had done – and they were in absolute awe of Him. They realized how great and mighty He was and how small and insignificant they were – and they melted in His presence, willingly offering Him His rightful position on the throne of their lives because they fully understood He was their Messiah, Savior, and Lord. They had a similar experience to what Isaiah had in Isaiah 6 – they were overwhelmed and humbled before God. So, they respectfully responded to Jesus as their resurrected Savior by loving Him with all of their heart, mind, soul, and strength.

This does raise a perplexing question, is it possible to worship and yet not be a worshiper? Yes, it is possible! Every person, in every generation, has been wired for worship; and we will all worship someone or something. It is the reality of the human condition – we cannot help it! Just watch a college or professional football game, and you can see worship in action. Yet, just because someone worships, this does not mean they are a worshiper of God; we all are capable of worshipping anyone or anything. Furthermore, there are degrees of worship. We can watch our favorite football team, wear their colors and logo, tailgate, and even cheer when they do well, and this all falls under the activity of worship. Yet as soon as the game is over, and we turn our attention to something else, we have just revealed that while we might have been engaged in the act of worship, we are not truly worshipers *because a worshiper would be radically abandoned and sold out to the team*. A true worshiper lives, eats, breaths, and sleeps it. Instead, our casual approach reveals that while we go to the game, and yell our support, we are really not worshipers – just fans!

A worshiper is on a different level than a person who occasionally worships. A worshiper is consumed and immersed because

---

[12] Information from www.preceptaustin.org

worship is not something we do – it is who we are. We have drunk the proverbial Kool-Aid. When a person becomes a worshiper, they become consumed with the object of their worship. It does not just become the driving force of their life – it is their life! This is what occurred that wonderful evening for those fortunate few on the mountain, they were transformed from a people who worshiped to a people who became worshipers much like the women at the well in John 4, the woman who anointed Jesus with perfume in Luke 7, and the Apostle Paul in Acts 9.

ME OR THEE

Which brings us back to our initial premise. *Every heart has a throne and every throne has a God or god.* Either the big-G God is sitting on the throne or the little-g god of self is sitting on the throne; but make no mistake, there is someone or something sitting on your heart's throne calling the shots and inspiring your motivation. When we boil it all down, we are either going to be a worshiper of God or a worshiper of ourselves. Either Jesus will sit on the throne or we will sit on the throne – and sadly, most people prefer to worship and serve themselves. Let me say this in a different way. No matter how much we attempt to spiritualize and baptize our wants, preferences, and desires, the only being we are serving is ourselves. We are making self the center of our universe expecting God to be in orbit around us. Just because a person says they are a Christian, it does not mean they are a worshiper. Just because we go to church, sing a few songs of praise, and raise our hands; it does not mean we are true worshipers. Just because we serve in a ministry, go on a mission trip, and talk the church lingo, it does not mean we are worshipers. Worship is more than reading our Bibles, giving money to help the ministry, and talking our faith; worship is having Jesus as the true object of our affections enthroned in our lives. Why? It is because the moment we make worship about our wants, preferences, and desires, instead of about honoring and submitting to God, we are no longer worshipping God but ourselves.

Think about it this way. In our universe, everything revolves around the sun. There was a time when people thought the sun revolved around the earth. If that were the case, our solar system would have collapsed. The same idea applies here. When we make worship about us instead of about God, we put ourselves on the throne and expect God to be in orbit around us, and we tend to live in the expectation that God exist to serve us – which is upside-down – and life collapses.

By the way, were you aware that ever since the fall, this has been the plight of man? We want God to serve us instead of the other way around. It is here we discover what sin is. Sin is the activity, attitude, and ambition we engage and embrace to ensure we are king of the hill in our lives and that God responds to our beck and call. Sin occurs because we choose ourselves as the rightful one to sit on the throne expecting God to orbit around our wants and wishes – which leads us to choose a way that seems right to ourselves that is always concerned and consumed with our wants, comforts, and convenience. Suffice to say, any time we choose sin, we are choosing to worship something or someone other than God.

Everything changes when we abdicate the throne in our lives to allow God to sit on the seat that He created within us for Himself. The odd and amazing truth is, God established this throne so that our lives would work and so our lives would bring glory and honor to Him. Yet since the fall, all we have experienced is a brutal tug-of-war battle within us, and within humanity, that has plagued us into a death-struggle with eternal and earthly con-sequences. This leaves us either to worship self or to deny self to worship God. If we choose ourselves, then we will love ourselves with all of our heart, mind, soul, and energy – and we will use others to gratify our wants and needs. If we choose to worship God, then we will love God with all of our heart, mind, soul, and strength, and it will spill over in how we engage and treat others.

In worship, a true disciple is choosing to give Jesus His rightful place and position on the throne of our lives and then allowing every area and detail of our lives to be overwhelmingly influenced and aligned to His will and way. In so doing, a disciple is giving God their mind's attention, their heart's affection, their will's ambition, and their life's actions. In this way, worship is not something we do as a disciple, it is who we are – and it affects everything we do and everyone we encounter. It will influence *why* we live, *how* we live, and for *whom* we live. Disciples worship because they have become worshipers, and because they are worshipers, everything they do will be an act of worship aimed at pleasing God and putting a smile on His face. So, if we have become a worshiper, then with joy, we will willingly engage in pursuing God because we realize God has allowed these opportunities to afford us the chance to express our love and affection to Him.

BECOMING A LIVING SACRIFICE

When does a person become a worshiper? On the mountain, when Jesus appeared to the eleven and everyone else present, they were transformed when they *saw Jesus fully for who He was and understood what He had done* – and it resulted in their faithful alignment and complete surrender. In that moment, they ceased being people who came to attend worship and they became worshipers who offered their lives to live on mission – submitted and surrendered to who Jesus was and for what He did. Romans 12:1-2 speaks into this idea:

> I urge you, brothers, in view of God's mercy, to offer your bodies as living sacrifices, holy and pleasing to God, this is your spiritual act of worship. Do not conform any longer to the pattern of this world, but be transformed by the renewing of your mind, then you'll be able to test and approve what God's will is, his good, pleasing and perfect will.

Paul was saying that when a person has truly experienced the glory and redeeming mercy of God, when they have genuinely come face-to-face with grace – they cannot help but to bend their knee, bow their hearts, surrender their will and offer their lives as a living sacrifice that is pleasing to God.

Consider the word *offer* (*paristasis*). It is the same word used of a priest who would offer a spotless lamb on an altar as a sacrifice for the forgiveness of sin.[13] The intent was not just to seek forgiveness; it was to realign his heart with God offering his life to God as an act of worship.

Now pay close attention, as this is why pastors learn Greek. The word here is not referring to a commitment a person makes over and over, but to a once-and-for-all transaction. In other words, we are not to be people who worship, leave, return, and then repeat the same inconsistent life pattern. Instead, in becoming a worshiper, we are to say, "God, here is my life; it is Yours to do with however you wish. I am a living sacrifice for your glory; and I will not ever take it back."

Let me offer an example. Dr. Glen Weekley, the former pastor at First Baptist Church of Hendersonville, Tennessee served as my Doctoral Field Supervisor. At the time, he was recovering from a kidney transplant donated to him by his daughter to save his life. I found it interesting that when she gave him her kidney, she did not give it to him expecting him to return it when he was done using it. She understood it was a once-and-for-all commitment and that there was no going back. She did not say, "Dad, here's my kidney, but I'm going to want it back in a year." She gave of herself to give life to her dad knowing it required her surrender.

This is a completely different disposition than many of us have as it pertains to following Jesus and loving Him with all of our heart, mind, soul, and strength. If we are honest, we tend to be a little more conditional and casual in our approach to following Jesus. Yet up until that moment on the mountain in Galilee, the men and women present probably were similar. But something happened that day that transformed their lives forever. Something occurred that caused them to surrender their lives to honoring God in everything they said and did for the rest of their lives. Something happened that caused them to understand that once-and-for-all Jesus was their Lord and Savior, and there would be no turning back.

---

[13] Information from www.preceptaustin.com

Additionally, we learn in this passage that the essential ingredient to worship is seeing Jesus for who He was as God in the flesh and believing that he died on the cross and arose from the grave – such conviction should change us forever. It should instill in us an unwavering affection for God that willingly gives Him His rightful place on the throne of our lives.

This brings us back to our key truth. *If every heart has a throne and every throne has a God or god* – then we need to make a once-and-for-all decision about what we are going to do with Jesus. First, we can sit on the proverbial throne and say, "Thanks God, but I got this. I can do this thing called life all by myself." Second, we can say, "Come here God and sit beside me. Be my co-pilot. I will steer and navigate – and You can bless." Or third, we can say, "Here Jesus. Here is the throne of my life. I will surrender all to you! And with every fiber of my affection, I will trust you with all of my heart and allow you to direct my steps – I will follow You!

CHAPTER 9

THE AUTHORITY OF GOD

When we oppose God's delegated authority,
we oppose God Himself.
John Bevere

THERE IS A humorous story about a government surveyor charged with going into the hollows of Kentucky to survey farmland in search of mineral and oil rights. As you can imagine, the landowners were not too keen on his visit. At one particular farm, the farmer was putting up a valiant fight, until the surveyor pulled out his official paperwork and told the farmer he had full government authority to go wherever he wanted and needed, and if the famer did not cooperate, he could be fined or taken to jail. Seemingly giving in, the farmer opened his gate to allow the surveyor into his pasture. But as the surveyor was setting up his equipment, the farmer went to the opposite end of the field and released his biggest, most vicious bull. Of course, within minutes, the bull had cornered the surveyor. When the surveyor began running and screaming for his life, the farmer yelled, "Show him your paperwork! Show him your paperwork. He will care about your authority as much as I do."

Authority can be tricky. Too much authority can lead to an abuse of power, while too little authority can leave a person vulnerable and powerless. When Jesus spoke of His authority, He was speaking of His sovereign Lordship and ability, and of His capability to empower others. When Matthew wrote, "*All authority in heaven and earth has been given to me...,*" he was implying that He was making His authority and power accessible to His followers so that they could effectively walk with God and accomplish His Great Commission.

MIGHT AND RIGHT

The authority of Jesus is an important influence to understand in the life of a disciple. The term Jesus used for authority (*exousia*), refers to having the might and the right to act and speak as one pleases.[14] Within the context of the passage, Jesus declared to his followers that based of who He was (God), what He had accomplished on the cross, He possessed supreme dominion and sovereignty over all things. Furthermore, He was imbued with the right to use this power whenever, wherever, and however He so desired or deemed worthy. In Colossians 1:15-20, the Apostle Paul offered a brief theological discourse to provide us with an insightful explanation of Jesus' rule and sovereign authority:

> The Son is the image of the invisible God, the firstborn over all creation. For in him all things were created: things in heaven and on earth, visible and invisible, whether thrones or powers or rulers or authorities; all things have been created through him and for him. He is before all things, and in him all things hold together. And he is the head of the body, the church; he is the beginning and the firstborn from among the dead, so that in everything he might have the supremacy. For God was pleased to have all his fullness dwell in him, and through him to reconcile to himself all things, whether things on earth or things in heaven, by making peace through his blood, shed on the cross.

As the agent of the Trinity in creation, the physical representation of God, Jesus possesses absolute sovereignty over the

---

[14] Information from www.preceptaustin.com

creation. So, as He stood before His disciples that day, it was fully within Jesus' might and right to imbue them with His power to accomplish His mission. Without limitations or restrictions, Jesus invited them to plug into His power and to go forth under His authority. He could offer this because there is no area outside of His purview and universal authority because Jesus alone possesses absolute power and the right to exercise this authority as He wills, namely because He had died for sin and had risen from the grave. Paul explained this well in Philippians 2 when he wrote:

> God has exalted Him and given Him a name that is above every name so that at the name of Jesus every knee shall bow in heaven and earth, and every tongue confess that Jesus Christ is Lord, to the glory of the Father. Philippians 2:9-11

This is just another way of saying, *"All authority in heaven and earth has been given to Me."* Not only did Jesus possess it as God, He earned it through His sacrifice and resurrection.

POWER UP

A cursory review of Jesus' life and ministry reveals that Jesus showed authority in a number of ways pertinent to our lives. First, Jesus showed us His authority over nature. We see this authority when He spoke creation into existence, when He walked on water, when He calmed the storm, and a number of other instances in the gospels. He also showed His authority over disease by giving sight to the blind, sound to the deaf, stamina to the lame, and skin to the leper. He showed His authority over the demonic by overcoming Satan in the wilderness, by closing the mouths of demons, and by casting demons into swine. He showed His authority over sin. A good example of this occurred when He gave grace to the woman caught in adultery. Do you remember His words to her? Jesus said, *"Where are your accusers? Neither do I accuse you. Go and sin no more."*

We learn in Scripture that Jesus, and NO ONE ELSE, possesses all authority time and space; over Satan and the demonic, and over the angelic realm. He has authority over all creation – over natural laws, objects, and forces – and over the sun, moon, stars, and planets. He has authority over gravity, thermodynamics, and Newton's first and second laws. He has dominion over the molecular and biological – over protons, neutrons, electrons, quantum physics, and DNA; He welds authority over all things living – plants, animals, the fish in the sea, the birds of the air, and all mankind. He has supremacy over every heartbeat, every breath, every electrical jump across a million brain synapses; over disease, bacteria, viruses, parasites, and germs. He has authority over the nations – over presidents, kings and legislatures, as well as over courts and justices, armies and wars. Jesus has authority over every soul and every moment within every life that has ever been or will be. Let that soak in. He alone possesses and is holy, worthy of this sovereign authority.

In returning to His statement to His disciples that day, when Jesus said, *"I possess all authority in heaven and earth,"* He was saying that He alone has been imbued with all power for one purpose – to accomplish the will of the Father. In this statement, He was implying two things: First, because He alone possesses this authority, the command He was giving to His disciples, they were to obey in every way. Second, He was telling them (and us) that the only way this command can be fulfilled is through His power and authority that is made accessible through the Holy Spirit. Thus, to experience His authority requires we know Him as our Savior and submit to Him as our Lord living in an abiding intimacy under the influence of the Holy Spirit.

Without question, this is ginormous! Because of who He is and what He has done, Jesus possesses absolute, sovereign authority to rule and do however He pleases – and He pleases to empower His people to go to the nations to live and proclaim the good news of His death, burial, and resurrection so that everyone might hear this good news and come into a relationship with Him. His disciples are His hands, feet, and voice to the nations to spread His love and share His amazing grace.

ABIDING IN HIS POWER

Access to His power only comes by way of the ministry of Holy Spirit. It begins with salvation and continues in a person's daily surrender and alignment with the Holy Spirit. Consider what Jesus said to His disciples in John 15:4-5:

> Abide in me, as I also Abide in you. No branch can bear fruit by itself; it must remain in the vine. Neither can you bear fruit unless you remain in me. "I am the vine; you are the branches. If you remain in me and I in you, you will bear much fruit; apart from me you can do nothing.

Whether we know this or not, or have accepted this truth or not, independently of God, we are all powerless and impotent to do anything to impress Him apart from His help and guidance. Why? Because God is not impressed with what our flesh can do and accomplish. He is only moved by what He can do in and through us by the Holy Spirit. This is contrary to our human nature that assumes total responsibility for pursuing life. Yet in our flesh, we can do nothing to please God. This is why Isaiah wrote, *"All of our righteous deeds are like filthy garments…"* He was helping us to see that in our human power, ability, and ingenuity, we can do nothing to impress or assist God. So, God came up with a better plan. Instead of us operating under our limited power, He wants us to operate in His limitless power and authority.

Consider Luke 9:1-2. When Jesus called and sent the Twelve out in pairs in His name. Luke says that Jesus, *"…gave them His power and authority to drive out all demons and to cure diseases, and he sent them out to proclaim the kingdom of God and to heal the sick."* Notice, Jesus did not send them out in *their* ability, but in His ability. He gave them His dynamic power and His authority so they would have the *might* needed to do it and the *right* (authority) to use it.

In Acts 1:8, Jesus did the same for us when He said, "But you will receive power when the Holy Spirit comes upon you; and you will be my witnesses in Jerusalem, in all Judea and Samaria, and to the ends of the earth." This passage reminds us that we do not go into the world under our power because it will not work. We go in God's power and authority, because it is the only power that can rescue and transform lives. Suffice to say, God never intended for the Christian life to be powered by our abilities and effort, but by the Holy Spirit dwelling in us seeking to live through us.

Have you ever been in a third world country? Whenever I have had the privilege of traveling to one of these countries, I have experienced a power outage at least twice a day. In many third-world countries, the power grid is inconsistent. In the same way, no matter how powerful we might think we are, we will experience power outages (blackouts) when we try to live life under our human power and ability. What God is saying to His followers in this statement is that when we live in His authority and under the influence (plugged into) of the Holy Spirit, we will never experience a blackout or loss of power.

Imagine that the power you possess within your flesh is a nine-volt battery. Would you have *some* power? Yes. But not much! Maybe enough to power a pocket radio or smoke alarm, but you are powerless to crank a car or power a jet. You would have limited power. The same is true for us spiritually. We might have some human ability, but life and the Great Commission can only be powered by the dynamic energy of the Holy Spirit in us living through us. Our lives are the conduit by which God accomplishes His will. Unfortunately, such truth is seldom taught. We continue to hear about how to train our flesh to be good instead of how to walk in the Spirit and in the power of God.

How do we live an abiding life in Jesus' authority? It occurs when we reside in the Holy Spirit who indwells us at the point of salvation and fills us in our daily surrender (see Ephesians 1:13 and 1 Corinthians 6:19). As we submit to His presence, and align our lives to His will and Word, we are allowing the ministry of the Holy Spirit to be released in our lives. In fact, our faith only works when we are plugged into God.

Dr. Tony Evans once offered a perfect illustration on what it means to abide and live plugged into the authority of God.

Suppose you go to buy a refrigerator. As you are browsing, you find the mack-daddy of refrigerators. Built-in TV, individual cooling zones – it has all the bells and whistles and more. Yet despite that it cost more than a normal refrigerator, you buy it anyway because of its features. Of course, once it has been delivered, you stock it with your favorite groceries and go about your business. But then something happens. Hours later, when you go to get a snack, you discover the milk has spoiled, the ice cream has melted, and water from the ice maker is leaking onto the floor – and you realize that your new refrigerator is not working. So, you call Best Buy for help; and the employee asks you to put your ear to the fridge to see if you can hear the hum of the motor – but there is no hum. He asks you to open the door to see if there is a light inside – but there is no light. So, he has you to pull the refrigerator away from the wall to see if it is plugged in – and it is not. But instead of accepting it, you say, "But this is a $5,000 refrigerator. It ought to work whether it is plugged in or not. To which the employee says, "It doesn't matter if it cost $5 or $5,000, all refrigerators are dependent appliances relying on an invisible, outside power source known as electricity to ensure it works.[15]

As God's children, we are completely dependent on God's influence in us through the Holy Spirit for our lives to work. The power of the Christian life does not come from us, it comes from God. This is why Solomon invited us to trust in the Lord with all of our hearts instead of in our own understanding and ingenuity.

Based on Jesus' words to His disciples in John 15, as Jesus followers, we must live in absolute dependence upon the Holy Spirit to power our lives. Our spiritual lives will not work unless they are plugged into the Holy Spirit – that requires our submission to God's authority in our lives. The Christian life is not something a person can do in their own ability and ingenuity; it can only be lived by allowing God's ability and power to work in and through us. Our job is to live submitted and under the influence of the Holy Spirit so that He can move and work through our lives for

---

[15] Tony Evans, *The Promise of the Holy Spirit*, (Chicago: Moody Press, 2002).

the glory of God. Bottomline, the Christian life cannot work apart from the indwelling and in-filling of the Holy Spirit.

Let us look at this from a different angle. If we were to search the Scripture from Genesis to Revelation, we will quickly discover there is not one verse in the Bible where God says believers can live independently of the Holy Spirit relying on their own talents, abilities, or ingenuity. Not one! In fact, it is just the opposite. Time and again, we read verses inviting us to trust in the Lord, lean not on your own understanding, deny yourself, and walk in the Spirit. Each of these passages speak to the truth that God empowers us to do His will. What we can never forget is God will always empower us to do His will, but He will never empower us to ignore His will for a way that seems right to ourselves. In abiding in Christ, we are choosing to live under His authority and in alignment with His will and way to allow God's power to make us adequate for His service.

HIS ADEQUACY IN US

I have always enjoyed the story of two milk cows who were eating grass when a milk truck drove by with a sign reading, "Fresh milk. Fortified. Homogenized. Pasteurized. Vitamin-enriched." After reading the descriptions, one cow said to the other, "It kinda makes you feel inadequate, doesn't it?"

Can you imagine how inadequate the disciples must have felt when they heard this command from Jesus' lips? I can just imagine Peter saying, "But Lord, we're just eleven ordinary men – we have no money, no means, or ability to fulfill this calling. We might be able to make a dent here in the Galilee, but I'm not so sure we can impact the nations? We can't we stand before the might of Rome or argue with the intelligence of the Greeks? Lord, we can't do it!" And Jesus replied, "You are right! You cannot; but I can through you! You cannot; but I will go with and before you. This is why I am giving you my power and authority."

The phrase, *as we go,* means we are not going in the name of our denomination or church, or even in our own name; we are going in His name, in the name that is above every name.

Furthermore, we are going in His authority and power and not in our ability or adequacy. When we submit to His authority, and allow His presence and power to be released in and through our lives, the Holy Spirit is released to do what only He can do – change lives!

Let me ask a question to explain. What is our role in the Great Commission? Is it to *convict* people? No! Is it to *convince* people? No! Is it to *convert* people? Nope! All of this is the work of the Holy Spirit. Our role is to go into the world and into our sphere of influence to *convey* the truth as God leads us. John Stott explained this well.

> His authority on earth allows us to dare to go to all the nations. His authority in heaven gives us our only hope of success. And His presence with us leaves us no other choice.[16]

He was explaining that following Jesus hinges on our willingness to submit to His authority and to align our lives to the leading of the Holy Spirit – anything less, and we are operating under our power instead of in His power. To be a disciple requires living under the influence of the Holy Spirit and plugged into His power.

---

[16] Stuart Strachan Jr., "Sermon Quotes", www.thepastorsworkshop.com.

CHAPTER 10
THE AGENDA OF GOD

This is God's Universe, and God does things His way.
You may have a better way, but you don't have a universe.
Vernon McGee

HAVE YOU HEARD the phrase, "Famous last words?" There is a cute story of a man who lost his wise, elderly father to cancer. A friend wanting to console him asked, "Your dad was so wise. I have to know, what were your dad's final words?" The son replied, "Dad did not have any last words. Mother was with him until the end."

When it comes to famous last words, the final recorded words of Jesus to His disciples in Matthew 28:19-20, just might be the most famous words in human history:

> ...go and make disciples of all nations, baptizing them in the name of the Father, Son and Holy Spirit, and teaching them to obey all I have commanded you. Matthew 28:19-20

These familiar words encompass what is better known as the Great Commission, which is the mission Jesus left His followers to fulfill so that every person, from every tribe and nation, might hear and receive the good news that *God so loved the world He gave His only begotten Son...*

This commission is paramount to the purpose and mission of the church – this is why the church exists. Everything a church does from corporate worship to mission engagement, to biblical instruction from the pulpit, in small groups, and life to life, must be measured and filtered by this Divine mandate. So, it is critical every Jesus-follower has clarity to this calling.

There is evidence that many Christians and churches may have some misunderstanding of the actual commission because they have mistaken participles for verbs. Let me ask you, "How many commands do you see in this passage? Take a moment to re-read the passage above and count the commands. How many did you count? Did you count four? Three? How many? Most people think there are four commands – *go*, *make*, *baptizing*, and *teaching*. But that would be inaccurate. In the Greek, there is only one. Can you guess it? It is not *go*! It is *make* disciples! The only verb in this passage in the Greek is *matheteuo* – *make disciples*. All the other words are participles explaining what is needed to make disciples.

Understanding this Greek word is critical to knowing Christ and living out the Great Commission. As previously discussed, the charge is not solely about conversion as many seem to teach; it is about making obedient, converted followers of Jesus who repro-duce themselves to the nations. When we make disciples, we are engaged in the mission of assisting people to have genuine belief in God marked by obedient followship to God. Therefore, baptizing and teaching are not separate jobs, they are necessary aspects to help a person genuinely know and follow Jesus.

One of the best examples of this truth is found in the story of the rich, young ruler in Luke 18. If you are unfamiliar with the story, a rich, moral guy came to Jesus wanting to confirm he had eternal life. He wanted enough of Jesus to be saved, but not enough to relinquish control of His life to Jesus. Obviously, he wanted salvation, yet he did not want to have to surrender his wants and will to follow. So, when Jesus laid down the gauntlet of genuine faith and followship, the Bible says the young man turned and walked away because ultimately, He wanted to follow God on his terms instead of on God's terms. He wanted salvation without surrender and Christ without commitment.

May I be blunt? Church rolls everywhere are filled with people like the rich, young ruler. They are people who want enough of Jesus to be saved, but not enough to live submitted to His Lordship. They are people who will claim to know Him, but whose lives say differently. Yet according to Jesus, if a person says they have faith, yet they are unwilling to follow, or if they say they believe, yet they do not have a desire to obey, then unfortunately, these people are not true Christians. They may be religious, go to church, or even, acknowledge there is something different about Jesus – but Jesus would say such an individual does not really know Him! Just because we might know about Him, it does not mean we really know Him! Why? Because *a disciple is a person so convinced Jesus was who He said He was and did what He said He would do that they trust and obey.* John MacArthur said it well when he wrote, "A true convert is a disciple – a person who has accepted and submitted their life to Christ – whatever that may mean or demand."[17] Vance Havner said the same thing only in a slightly different manner:

> Salvation is free... and the gift of God is eternal life. It's not cheap for it cost God His Son and the Son His life, but is free to those who believe. However, when we become true believers, we become disciples – and that'll cost everything we have. Lest we forget, our Lord was after disciples – not mere joiners.[18]

The bottomline is, if you do not believe Jesus is your Lord and Savior enough to actually *live* it, it is likely because, deep down, you do not really believe it. Genuine faith believes and obeys. Which brings us to the three Great Commission participles and what is involved in making a person who trusts and obeys.

---

[17] John MacArthur, The MacArthur New Testament Commentary, John 1-11, (Chicago: Moody Press, 2008).

[18] www.vancehavner.com.

DISCIPLES SERVE THE WORLD

The Great Commission is God's plan for rescuing the nations from the problem of sin. It is His way of sharing hope and offering grace through our willing witness. You may not agree this is the best method to share the Good News, but it is God's plan. Entrusting His people with His message and empowering them with His love is His plan to address mankind's need for grace. Our participation is essential. Attributed to Hudson Taylor, he said, "The Great Commission is not an option to be considered; it is a command to be obeyed.[19] Because God's people living and sharing His love and grace is the best way to get the word out.

The Great Commission begins with *going,* as in, *as you are going*... Jesus shared this idea with the expectation that His life in us would be on the move through us. We are to be going with the intent of serving others to Jesus to earn the right to speak with them about the hope that is within us.

The word *go* is a participle of assumption. Because we have trusted Jesus as our Savior and Lord, and had our lives transformed by His grace, *as we are going* about our lives, intersecting with the nations, we must be ready to jettison our holy huddles to venture into the highways and byways of everyday life to live on mission for Jesus to make disciples of everyone we meet. The idea is to live moment-by-moment, in the normal traffic patterns of life, consciously aware we are witnesses to the love and grace of God.

So, *going into the world to make disciples* is so much more than going on a mission trip. It is consciously living on mission in the everyday aspects of our lives. At work. At school. At home. At church. At the ball field. On an airplane. At the store. In your car. It is living compelled to help others see and experience the same Jesus who has rescued and transformed your life. Let us reconsider Paul's encouragement to the Corinthians mentioned earlier.

---

[19] Matthew Schmalz, "What is the Great Commission and Why is it so Controversial", www.christianitytoday.com, February 2019.

> For Christ's love compels us, because we are
> convinced that one died for all, and therefore
> all died. And he died for all, so that those who
> live should no longer live for themselves but for
> Him who died for them and was raised again. 2
> Corinthians 5:14-15

Notice the word, *compels*. The idea is that God's love *in us* moves us to a single focus to live for Him. We are so moved by the resurrection in us we are motivated to share with others the hope within us. Furthermore, what compels us is Christ in us. We do not go in our name, or in our power, ability, or adequacy, we go in His name and under the influence of the Holy Spirit. We go listening for the Holy Spirit to lead and guide us to show us where God is at work and how we are to minister in His name.

Paul was explaining that the Great Commission begins with a *go and tell* mentality and not with a *come and hear* mentality. We go, in the prompting and guidance of the Holy Spirit, to serve others to Jesus by sharing the Good News through our actions and words. Note that it requires actions and then words, teaching us that it is more critical to walk your faith than it is to talk your faith. Or as the old adage goes – *"Share Jesus always, when necessary... use words!"* This is in no way passive. We intentionally live our faith to earn the right to talk our faith.

This reminds me of an encounter I had several years ago, when I was traveling with a young man from Richmond, Virginia to the New River Gorge in West Virginia to go whitewater rafting on the Gauley River. As we were traveling, unsolicited, he shared with me that he did not believe in God. In that moment, I remember having an overwhelming sense the reason he had no conviction of God was because he had a skewed view of who God and Jesus were. After he took a few minutes describing his view of God, I said, "I have been a Christian for a while, and what you just described is not the God I know. May I introduce you to the God of the Bible?" After he agreed, I started at the beginning and took Him from creation, to the cross, and ultimately, to the empty tomb. When I finished, before I could ask him if he wanted to know Christ as His Savior and Lord, he said, "Now that's the kind of God I would like to know and have a relationship with. Can you help me to know Him?" Of course, I responded, "Why yes... yes I can!" So, we pulled onto the shoulder on Interstate 81, and he prayed to accept Christ as His Savior and Lord and was later baptized at our church.

DISCIPLES SHOW THE WORD

Speaking of baptism, the term *baptizing* refers to being fully immersed or submerged in fluid or stained with a dye. Baptism is a symbolic gesture used by the church to identify someone whose life had been transformed by the grace of God. In many ways, it is a liquid brand or invisible, spiritual tattoo to bear witness that a person has received Christ as their personal Savior and Lord. In this instance, it is referring to the act of baptism, and to the entire transaction of salvation from the moment a person hears the good news, until they believe, and then follow in baptism. In the Great Commission, Jesus is calling His disciples to participate in living and speaking the salvation story of God. Meaning, the role of a disciple is to live on mission ready to share with others the Good News that God so loved them He gave His life to rescue them from the wages of their sin. But we are to do more than just convey the message, we are to participate in helping people who confess and believe to grow to maturity. We are charged with walking alongside of them to spur them on in the faith.

In the context of the Great Commission, baptism refers to a person hearing the Word, then after believing it, they align their life by following Jesus through the displaying of their faith in the act of water baptism to give testimony that their life has been transformed by God's grace. The physical activity of baptism is intended to declare a person's genuine belief and commitment to following Jesus. It is a physical gesture to illustrate and testify to the spiritual transaction that has taken place at salvation. Consider Paul's words in Romans 6:3-4:

Do you not know that all of us who were baptized into Christ were baptized into his death? Thus, we were buried with him through baptism into death in order that, just as Christ was raised from the dead thru the glory of the Father, we too may live a new life.

This was and is a big deal! In the early church, a person did not get baptized if they did not believe because to get baptized was to identify with Christ and to put their life in danger. In a culture of persecution, this would have been tantamount to signing your own death certificate. If you did not mean it, then you would not have done it because of what was at stake. Which brings us to the third and final aspect of the Great Commission – *teaching them to obey all I have commanded you...*

DISCIPLES SOW THE WAY

As we go, we are also called to plant the truths of God in others by investing the lessons Jesus has taught us into them until they are able to feed on God for themselves. We are to teach others how to trust and obey – and how to see, hear, and experience God through the Holy Spirit, so they too can live on mission and share God's love.

The phrase, *teaching them to obey*, refers to our charge to assist people in walking in obedience to God's will and Word by living in alignment with the Holy Spirit so that He can guide their lives and direct their steps. The word used here for *teaching* means to cause to know or to help others to learn the content and intent, and also how to put it into practice. It refers to a choir director who trains a choir over a long period of rehearsals until they know the music and cues so thoroughly and intimately by heart, they can perform the piece flawlessly from memory. Meaning the music has become a part of them.[20]

---

[20] Information found at www.preceptausting.org

Teaching people to obey requires incarnational and informational instruction. One of my mentors would say teaching people to obey all that Jesus commanded requires intentional *relational* interaction and intentional *revelational* instruction. In other words, to help someone to know and walk with Jesus requires life-to-life, personal alongsiding where truth is shared, discussed, processed, and practiced. This is at the heart of Paul's words in 2 Timothy 2:2, "The things you have seen and heard in me, these entrust into reliable men who will be qualified to teach others also." Paul encouraged his protégé to walk and dialogue with these reliable leaders to show them the way so they might know the way.

This is our commission. We are to go into our small part of the world, ready to be used by God, to share with others the hope that is within us so that others might also follow Him. It is a call to participate in helping the world to hear and receive the good news that God loves them and gave His life to rescue and redeem them.

In considering the Great Commission, the story of the Coca-Cola Company offers some perspective of its possibility. In 1886, a pharmacist by the name of Dr. John Pemberton, concocted a caramel-colored syrup in a brass kettle in his backyard that he began selling on May 8, 1886 at Jacob's Pharmacy in downtown Atlanta. For nearly 90 years, Coke was an American drink. But in the early 1970's, the executives of Coke decided they wanted every person, on every continent, in every nation to taste the drink. Since then, Coke has become the most recognized brand and beverage in the world. Personally, I find it interesting that in their first year in 1886, they sold just 25 bottles – today the company sells 1.8 billion bottles per day with a market value of $203 billion. Furthermore, at this time, Coca-Cola is legally sold in every country in the world but one – North Korea.[21]

Imagine, in less than 50 years, the Coca-Cola Company has reached the world. It is interesting to think that if Jesus would have given the Great Commission to the Coca-Cola Company, the

---

[21] Information found at www.coca-cola.com.

gospel likely would have already been presented to every person on earth!" Only that is not what He chose to do. He gave it to His disciples (to His church) – to you and to me. Which raises an important question. Will we go into our corner of the world, into our everyday lives – to the places where we live, work, and play – to live what we say we believe before each and every person our lives intersect? Will we serve our family, friends and neighbors, our colleagues and customers to earn the right to help them to know Jesus as their Savior so they can walk with Him as their Lord? Anything less, and God's Great Commission will become our great omission.

CHAPTER 11

THE ASSURANCE OF GOD

The great basis of Christian assurance is not how much our hearts are set on God, but how unshakably His heart is set on us.
Tim Keller

YOU HAVE LIKELY heard the story of the man who all of his life, every time he got paid, took twenty dollars out of his paycheck and put it under his mattress. After over forty years, the man fell deathly ill. Realizing he was not going to survive, he called his wife to his bedside and said, "I want you to promise me one thing." She asked, "Promise what?" He said, "I want you to promise that when I have passed, you will take the money from under the mattress and put it in my casket so I can take it with me to my grave." On the day he passed, his wife kept her promise. She retrieved the money, deposited it to her bank account, and then, on the day of his funeral, she wrote a check and put it in his casket.

By definition, a promise is a sworn oath to assure someone you will fulfill what you have committed to do. It is a pledge, a guarantee, and a binding contract. God's promise is more. It is a covenant, and that is a promise on steroids. It is a promise bound in blood requiring an *oath of obligation* and a *walk into death*. It is a promise to keep your word or die trying. As Jesus finished his pep talk with those present on the mountain that marvelous day, He closed with a remarkable promise, *"Surely, I am with you always, to the end of the age."*

A PROMISE OF HIS PRESENCE

Throughout the Bible, God has made approximately 8,810 *promises*. Some 7,706 are found in the Old Testament, while the remaining 1,104 are in the New Testament. Of all the promises God has pledged, maybe none of them are as important as the promise Jesus made in Matthew 28:20 that He would be with His disciples always.

There is power in a promise made, and in a promise kept. On February 4, 1995, my wife and I made the most important earthly promise anyone can make when we vowed to love one another for better or for worse, for richer or for poorer, in sickness and in health, until death, do we part. Only we did not say the words, "I do." On that special day in Dallas, Texas, we said, "I promise." Inscribed inside her wedding band is my promise. And believe it or not, I even wrote a song for her entitled, "I Promise." The reason we chose these words was to align our vows with God's covenant promise. We wanted to be clear with our intentions that failure and divorce were not going to be an option, we were in this for the long haul.

In Matthew 28:20, Jesus offered His followers the unfailing promise of His presence with them. The reason God's promises are powerful is because He is obligated to keep His promises as a result of His holy nature. He can never be unfaithful to His commitments – it is not within Him. Here, in this often-forgotten verse, is one of the most important and powerful promises in the Bible. The words, "*I am with you always,*" is a promise of God's guiding and abiding presence and power to us.

Jesus' use of the personal pronoun, "*I,*" is not to be overlooked. In fact, it is to be cherished and remembered regularly, "*I will be with you.*" Consider that in this selection of words, the eternal Creator has promised that He would never leave His disciples. The One who flung the stars into place, who calmed the seas, and who rose from the dead, promised to walk before them and with them, through thick and thin, in good times and in challenging times. This promise coincides with Isaiah's words in Isaiah 41:10:

Do not fear, for I am with you; do not be dismayed, for I am your God. I will strengthen you and help you; I will uphold you with my righteous right hand.

God has promised His followers His *presence*, His *power*, His *protection*, His *provision* and His *purpose*. He has fully committed Himself to His followers just as He promised His presence to the Israelites during the exodus in Deuteronomy 31:6:

Be strong and courageous. Do not be afraid or terrified because of them, for the Lord your God goes with you; he will never leave you nor forsake you.

In delving deeper into Matthew 28:20, "*I will be with you always,*" means Jesus will be with you *without a break, all your days.* That is, He will be with us – *always and in all ways.* What a statement! God promised His disciples that as they went into the world that He was going to be with them always and in all ways. I am reminded of Psalm 121:1-7:

I lift up my eyes to the mountains – where does my help come from? My help comes from the Lord, the Maker of heaven and earth. He will not let your foot slip – He who watches over you will not slumber; indeed, the Lord who watches over Israel will neither slumber nor sleep. The Lord watches over you – the Lord is your shade at your right hand; the sun will not harm you by day, nor the moon by night. The Lord will keep you from all harm – He will watch over your life; the Lord will watch over your coming and going both now/ forevermore.

God's promise to His disciples, and to every person who follows Him, is that He would never leave or forsake them. He would never fall asleep at the wheel or slip into a slumber. He would never check out, go on vacation, or call in sick. God promised He would be present! He has promised His followers that as we go into our world to live on mission with Him, He will go with us, He will go ahead of us – and He will take care of us. And He did more than just promise His presence, He also promised to lead and guide us, to prompt us, so that we might accomplish His mission and live the Christian life.

THE FREQUENCY OF GOD

The promise of God to walk with us is to prompt and guide us in our pursuit of His will and mission. Essential to living in His promises is learning to distinguish His voice and leading in our lives. When we speak of the prompting of God, we are referring to the reality that God speaks into our lives by His Word and by His Holy Spirit to guide and direct our steps. This is not saying we audibly hear God's voice, rather that He speaks in a manner, and through a variety of resources, that connects with our mind, heart, and soul.

The idea of God speaking should not seem too mystical to us. Throughout Scripture, there are countless stories of God frequently speaking to His people. In the Old Testament, God spoke to and through the prophets. In the gospels, God spoke through Jesus. Now, since Pentecost, God speaks through the Holy Spirit. From Adam in Genesis to John in Revelation, God not only spoke, He spoke clearly to anyone who would listen. Thankfully, the same God who spoke in the pages of Scripture is still speaking today – and just as in the past, He speaks today because He wants us to personally know and accomplish His will and live in His abiding promise.

Hearing God is both harder than it sounds and easier than one might think. Harder, because it requires that we walk in faith and live surrendered to God's Word and will. Easier than one might think, because God has given us everything we need to thrive under the influence of the Holy Spirit if we will tune our hearts and minds to the tenor of His voice. Henry Blackaby wrote, "If a disciple doesn't know when God's speaking, he's in trouble at the heart of His Christian life!"[22] This is because the Christian life is about Christ in you – living through you. It is about knowing God, hearing His voice, and responding to His leading. This requires being in touch and in tune with God.

Knowing God refers to knowing Him as Savior in salvation and growing in intimacy with Him as Lord. *Hearing* God refers to cultivating a listening ear that is able to hear and distinguish God's voice in your everyday life so you can follow His leading. *Obeying* God refers to having a willing and responsive spirit to God's leading in your life so you can willingly do what He is asking you to do. A disciple strives to follow God's lead; they wait for God's stamp of approval. A disciple does not move until they know God is *in* it and *for* it, because they have tuned into the frequency of God to follow the Lord's leading to make certain God is *with* them. Which raises a relevant question, how does a person get on the correct frequency with God? The answer is simple – by being frequent with God.

Several years ago, while teaching on this topic, one of the funniest things to ever happen to me in the pulpit occurred. I had an old pre-digital radio on stage, plugged into the sound system. My plan was to start with static and then dial in 93.3 FM (our local Christian radio station). Instead of dialing left, I went right, and accidentally tuned into 94.1FM – and the song playing at the time was, *Do You Think I'm Sexy!* Yep... it was absolutely hilarious! As the congregation laughed uncontrollably, my only response was... "Why yes... Yes, I do think I'm sexy!" Needless to say, it certainly left an impression, and it made my point because until we learn to recognize and distinguish God's voice from the voice of our flesh, the voice of the world, and the voice of the enemy, we will likely miss God for our own will and plans.

---

[22] Henry Blackaby and Claude King, *Experiencing God*, (Nashville: Broadman and Holman, 1994).

THE WORD OF GOD

In the Bible, we learn there are three words regarding the prompting and voice of God – *logos, rhema,* and *hupakouo.* Each of these words speak to the Word and voice of God. Logos refers to the full counsel of Scripture applicable to everyone. It is God's truth for life and salvation. In 2 Peter 1:3-11, Peter explained that in Christ and in His Word, we find everything we need for life and godliness. Through the logos, God has revealed His truth to us along with the way of salvation and the guidelines of a disciple's life. The writer of Hebrews also speaks of the influence of the logos:

> For the word (logos) of God is alive and active. Sharper than any double-edged sword, it penetrates even to dividing soul and spirit, joints and marrow; it judges the thoughts and attitudes of the heart. Hebrews 4:12

The logos is God's tool to teach us right from wrong, good from evil, and what is of God and not of God. It is Truth that cuts to the heart of the matter and surgically works within us to eliminate anything in our lives that impedes our ability to know and walk with God. James wrote that the *logos* was also truth to confront us:

> Do not merely listen to the word (logos), and deceive yourselves. Do what it says. Anyone who listens to the Word but does not do what it says is like someone who looks at his face in a mirror and, after looking at himself, goes away and immediately forgets what he looks like. But whoever looks intently into the perfect law that gives freedom, and continues in it – not forgetting what they have heard, but doing it; they will be blessed in what they do. James 1:22-25

Comparing the logos to a mirror is a significant teaching. Just as a mirror reflects the reality of a person's exterior appearance, God's Truth is a true reflection of the inner person revealing the good, the bad, and the ugly within each of us. The logos is therefore essential truth to establish truth and to reveal to us who God is and what is necessary to have a relationship with Him. But God's voice does not stop at logos. God moves deeper and most specifically into our lives through *rhema*.

Rhema is truth realized by revelation special to you. It is God speaking logos directly into your life through the Holy Spirit to influence your daily life. It is God speaking directly into your situation to guide you to His will. Paul spoke about this in Romans 10:17, *"Faith comes from hearing and hearing by the word (rhema) of God."*

We do not often hear about rhema, yet rhema is the most essential aspect of God's voice because it is revelation specific to us. It is God speaking directly into our lives for us to know Him and not just know about Him. For example, it is one thing to read *"God loves you,"* and appreciate the sentiment, and completely another to realize that *God so loved you that He died for you.* In fact, the Scripture is concise in that a person cannot be delivered from their sin (saved) unless they experience the rhema of God to understand by revelation of the Holy Spirit that they are a sinner in need of a Savior. Rhema reveals and understanding that Jesus alone is the solution to the problem of sin. This is where conviction comes into play.

Let me illustrate this idea with one of my favorite stories. There was once a college literature professor who enjoyed traveling to county fairs where he would recite famous speeches and passages. With his deep, melodious voice, he would leave people spellbound by his flawless monologues. One evening, after finishing the Gettysburg address to a standing ovation, the professor asked the audience if they had any requests? An old pastor sitting in the back of the room asked if the professor would quote Psalm 23. Realizing something unique about this man, the professor agreed, but only if after he quoted it, the old pastor would quote it too. The professor began, *"The Lord is my shepherd I shall not want...*" and it was beautiful. Everyone in the room, hung on every word. When he concluded, the crowd erupted to a standing ovation. The professor then gave the floor to the pastor. As he approached the front, in a worn raspy voice from years of preaching, he began to speak from his heart: "*The Lord is my shepherd I shall not want. He makes me to lie down in green pastures. He leads me beside the still waters He restores my soul...*" As he completed the final words, "*Surely goodness and mercy will follow me all the days of my life and I will dwell in the house of the Lord forever,*" there was only stunned silence! No one spoke. No one moved. The only sound was that of people sniffling fighting back tears. As the old pastor sat down, the wise professor stood up and said, "Do you understand what just happened? Do you understand the difference? I know the 23rd Psalm; but friends, this man knows the shepherd!" The difference is rhema.

The third word regarding the voice of God is *hupakouo*. This word refers to truth heard, embraced, and lived. The word means to *hear under*. It is God calling us to follow His leading in our lives. It is our response to logos and rhema. It is what we do when God speaks – we obey. Consider Jesus' words to His disciples in John 10:27, "*My sheep hear (akouo) my voice. I know them, and they follow me.*" God speaks generally and then specifically into our lives with one expectation – that we put into practice whatever He reveals and asks us to do.

An oversimplified explanation of this truth is that God gives us *logos* that we might KNOW Him, *rhema* that we might HEAR Him, and *hupakouo* that we might OBEY Him. And God speaks through these various mediums because He seeks to prompt us to participate in *knowing* Him, *following* Him, and *serving* Him.

TUNING UP

A number of years ago, I witnessed an interesting phenomenon while skiing in France. As I was swishing down the mountain, I was surprised by a group of blind skiers. Yes, you heard me right. There was a group of visually impaired individuals skiing down an intermediate slope. Now, skiing is hard enough when you can see; I cannot imagine skiing without sight under the direction of someone else's voice. Apparently, this is not all that unusual. Ski guides use voice commands and a tapping technique with their ski poles to guide blind skiers down the hill. In spite of the wind and the clamor of other skiers, a blind skier has learned how to tune into and distinguish his guide's voice.

Let me offer another example. Often, when I am teaching on this idea with someone one-on-one over a coffee, I will have them take a moment to listen to all of the ambient noise around them that they were seemingly unaware of because they were so locked in on my voice. The people working, the other customers talking, the cars passing by outside, all seems to disappear when you get locked in on the one voice you are desiring to hear. The same is true with God.

How do we tune into God and live in His promise? First, we must *"be still and know that He is God."* In begins with quiet submission. Many of us are so busy and preoccupied with life, it is basically impossible for us to hear God for all the noise around us. The cares of the world, the pursuit of financial stability, and the desire for satisfaction holds too many of us hostage and tied in knots. Slowing down, settling in, and quieting our soul is essential for living in the assurance of God. As Rick Warren once said in a sermon, "An inner calm gives us an intercom to God."

Second, we must be desperately frequent with God. The key to being frequent with God is spending time with Him on a regular basis in His Word, in prayer, in worship, in community, and on mission. In this manner, we get in tune with God and become able to hear Him speak. As we begin to be frequent with God, we will find that we will get on the same wavelength with the Holy Spirit, and He will prompt us into His mission and will for our lives. The key is being able to distinguish God's voice from all of the other voices around including the voice of Satan and the demonic, the voice of the flesh, and the voice of the world.

Finally, we must be readily willing to respond when we hear God speak into our lives calling us to live out His promises. We must be surrendered to His will before our will and His way over our way. It is in having a willing spirit that God's Spirit is allowed to live and move in and through our lives as His disciples.

So, in this promise, *I will be with you always,* God is promising His disciples that He will be with us and for us. He is committing to prompt us so that our lives might live in His power, under His protection, with His provision, and for His purpose. This is the call of the disciple!

CHAPTER 12
PROPS TO GRANDPOP

*What you leave behind is not what is engraved in
stone monuments,but what is woven into the lives of others.*
Pericles

MY FIRST HERO in life was my Grandpa, Italo Frank Berta. After
God made him, the mold was broken. He was one of a kind. The
son of Italian immigrants, raised in Hell's Kitchen in New York City,
he was passionate about his family and as kind-hearted of a man
as you will ever meet. Not only was I named after him (my middle
name is Italo), I was fortunate to have been able to spend a lot of
quality time with him. I saw him at his best and at his worst – and
thankfully, most of the time, it was his very best.

When I was a young child and into my early teens, nearly
every Saturday morning, my Grandpa would pick me up early,
take me to breakfast at McDonald's, and then we would head to
the three or four grocery stores to get the next week's supplies
for my grandparents. Throughout our day, we would talk about
anything and everything, and enjoy a few laughs along the way.
Most of the time though, Grandpa would invest pearls of wisdom
and model how to engage and treat others. After four hours of
mentoring, the day would usually end with a Philly cheesesteak
and chocolate milkshake at Woolworth's and my Grandpa giving
me all of the change he had amassed throughout the day as a
weekly allowance.

What I remember most, and cherish still today, is my
Grandpa's interest and commitment to help me to become the

best man I could possibly become. He invested all of himself into me because he loved me and because my life would one day represent his legacy. He taught me about family, about life, about people, how to treat others, and about how to always give your very best effort. What did he do? He mentored me. He poured his values and convictions into me.

What was it about my Grandpa that made such a difference? It was his love for me and the personal investment of his life into my life. He coached me up-close-and personal. Grandpa did not rely on someone else to do it for him, he willingly took responsibility for my growth and development. This is what is required in making disciples.

Making disciples is not solely the responsibility of the church, nor is it solely the pastor's or deacon's responsibility. Making disciples is every believer's responsibility. It is our duty. Each of us is called to pour the Jesus in us into the life of other souls until they know Christ, and walk with Him, reproducing the Jesus in them into the lives of others too. For this to occur, we all must engage and do our part. We all need to create enough margin in our lives to make a difference in the life of someone else. Until this happens, the church will continue to experience decline. Until this happens, our families and friendships will continue to suffer the loss of spiritual vitality and maturity.

Several years ago, while pastoring in White House, Tennessee, I was fortunate to cross paths with a very influential disciple maker, Herb Hodges. Herb's influence impacted thousands of lives around the world for the sake of the gospel through his personal effort to make disciples. He was famous for promoting a downline strategy of disciple-making. That is, a disciple makes a disciple who makes a disciple... and so on.

His rationale was not only Jesus' method for making disciples, it was simple math. He would often ask, "Would you rather have a penny every day doubled for 30 days or $1 million? Choose quickly." If you selected the million dollars, you would have lost out on an additional $4,368,709.12. Why? Because things grow much faster when they compound!

In Jesus' model of making disciples, He presented a compounding strategy that has been lost on most churches today. Now to be sure, most churches want to experience numerical and spiritual growth, yet instead of following Jesus' example, we tend to launch out into a totally different direction. Instead of ministering life-to-life, we hold our big events and weekly worship services hoping someone will give their lives to Christ because of the words we speak, the music we sing, the videos we show, and the creativity we exhibit. And thankfully, we do hear about a few people turning to Christ, however, that does not mean we are truly making a Great Commission dent. In retrospect, Jesus trained His disciples not to focus on holding events, but to focus on doing life with others. He taught them how to invest personally into the lives of others more than He taught them to hold a rally or plan a retreat. Why? It is because Jesus understood that the gospel spreads farther and faster through a satisfied, abandoned follower than it does through an entertaining church event or program. Lest we forget, if the gospel is anything, it is personal.

So, let me encourage all of us (pastors, church leaders, and church attenders) to reconsider how we are pursuing ministry and what we prioritize as ministry. Thankfully, we are doing many things well and helpful to the Great Commission. Nonetheless, we must recognize what makes disciples and what supports the disciple-making process – and never confuse the two. We must keep the main thing the main thing. This will require that we take a step from behind our pulpits, walk off the platform, and begin ministering personally instead of just professionally. It will require that we focus more on the organic than the organizational. Furthermore, it will mean that our churches begin to focus on people more than on programs, parties, picnics, and even preaching. Yes, even preaching. If disciples make disciples, then preaching, while important, serves primarily to support the disciple-making process. Lest we forget, Great Commission ministry is about people and encouraging them into intimacy with the Savior. It is not about coddling people, but confronting and challenging them to pursue God's will for their lives. This brings us back to Paul's encouragement to his protégé Timothy.

The things you have heard me say in the presence of many witnesses entrust to reliable people who will also be qualified to teach others. 2 Timothy 2:2

I have been quite fortunate in life to have had a granddad who loved me and poured his life into me, and to have had a spiritual mentor, Carl, who poured the Jesus in him into me. Today, I continue to have spiritual mentors and mentees – and so should you. If you want to thrive in your pursuit of God, it will require allowing others into your life to encourage and to help shape your faith. It will require you choosing to walk alongside of others, life to life, to pour the Jesus in you into them. It only takes a little time, a little effort, and a willingness to get your hands dirty for you to make a significant impact on another life in Jesus' name. I can promise that you will be glad you did!

I wish you well in living out the Great Commission and hope to meet you somewhere along the journey.

BIBLIOGRAPHY

Bolsinger, Tod, Canoeing the Mountains, Downers Grove: InterVarsity Press, 2015.

Bonhoeffer, Dietrich, *The Cost of Discipleship*, Munich: Christian Kaiser Verlag, 1937.

Bonhoeffer, Dietrich, *Christ the Center*, Munich: Christian Kaiser Verlag, 1960.

Breen, Mike, *Building a Discipling Culture*, Pawley Island: 3DMovements, 2011.

Chambers, Oswald, *My Utmost for His Highest*, Grand Rapids: Discovery House, 1963.

Clarke, Chap, *The Performance Illusion*, Eugene: Wipf and Stock Publishers, 1993.

Coleman, Robert, *The Master Plan of Evangelism*, Grand Rapids: Revell, 1987.

Evans, Tony, *The Promise of the Holy Spirit*, Chicago, Zondervan, 2002.

Hodges, Herb, *Tally Ho the Fox*, Memphis: Spiritual Life Ministries, 2001.

Hull, Bill, *The Disciple-Making Pastor*, Grand Rapids: Baker Books, 1988.

MacArthur, John, *The MacArthur New Testament Commentary – Matthew 24-28*, Chicago: The Moody Bible Institute, 1989.

MacArthur, John, *The MacArthur New Testament Commentary – John 1-11*, Chicago: The Moody Bible Institute, 2008.

Mowry, Bill, *The Way of the Alongsider*, Colorado Springs, NavPress, 2012.

Schmalz, Matthew, "What is the Great Commission and Why is it so Controversial", www.christianitytoday.com, February 2019.

Strachan Jr., Stuart, "Sermon Quotes", www.thepastorsworkshop.com, 2020.

Vander Laan, Ray, *In the Dust of the Rabbi*, Grand Rapids: Zondervan, 2006.

Vander Laan, Ray, "Rabbi and Talmidim", www.thattheworldmay-know.com, 2021.

CPSIA information can be obtained
at www.ICGtesting.com
Printed in the USA
FSHW020729240321

9 781662 811814